Goal Boss

THE ART & SCIENCE OF
GETTING STUFF DONE

Will Pemble

CROC SMILE PRESS
NEW YORK • NEW YORK

Will Pemble/Croc Smile Press
300 East 34th Street, Suite 26A
New York, New York 10016
www.goalboss.com

Ordering Information:
Quantity sales. Special discounts are available on quantity purchases by corporations, associations, and others. For details, contact the "Special Sales Department" at the address above.

Goal Boss • The Art & Science of Getting Stuff Done / Will Pemble — 1st ed.
ISBN 978-0-9998143-0-7

Contents

Hi Mom!

This book is for you.
Please tape it to the fridge
where everyone can see!

Love,
Will

Acknowledgements

Thank you to my bride Liz! My sweet sweetie, who puts up with my kooky work and play, supporting my undying notion that we can live in the big house, travel the world, and goof off on weekdays. Liz simultaneously tethers me to reality and turns me loose to dream and create. She's the first person I look for in a crowded room.

Thank you to Ellie and Lyle, who taught me how to be a dad. They delight and challenge me every day, reminding me to bring a little parenting into everything I do.

Anthony is a rock star and a genius. Sometimes, I step outside myself and watch as he patiently explains the patently-obvious to me for third or fourth time. His contributions to this project show up on every page.

Lois made this book readable. She also raised me from a pup, which cannot have been easy. What a joy to add writing a book to our long list of projects. I love you, Mom!

Angela, Chris, Ivan, Kathy and Veev kept the wheels on the wagon all day, every day back in the day.

Thank you to my amazing clients, including without limitation Andy, Brian, Carena, Corey, Dave, Diane, Frank, Jim, Josh, Mike, Nick, Phil, Ralph, Rick, Shelly, Steve, Zach and so many others!

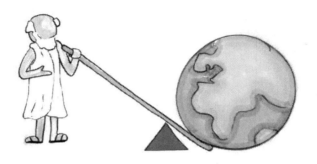

*Give me a place to stand and with a lever
I will move the whole world.*

—ARCHIMEDES

Death by Winning

Once upon a time, I built and sold Web.com, a company that started in my basement, and grew to be one of the Top 20 Domain and Web Hosting Companies in the world. I also built one of the first Internet Service Provider companies in San Francisco, and a successful Microsoft and Cisco certification training company with offices in San Francisco and Denver. Three companies, three exits. So far, so good.

My name is Will Pemble. I'm a certified technical trainer, a certified product manager, a certified flight instructor, leadership trainer, an executive coach, and I have a whole bunch of other certifications that objectively demonstrate that I am good at building companies, good at developing leaders, and good at connecting the dots when it comes to business. In my view, the best thing about business success is that it provides what we all need for what I call personal success. I am also the founder and CEO of Goal Boss. We will get into that any minute now.

I live with my wife and two kids in San Francisco, and we have homes in Connecticut, New York and Europe. Every year, we log roughly forty-five days of vacation as a family. One of my hobbies is building roller coasters. I've built five backyard roller coasters that have been featured on Good Morning America, Netflix, and dozens of other internationally recognized websites, blogs and television shows. I have been blessed with an extraordinary life.

But life wasn't always like this. Perhaps a good place to start would be with the story of how I almost didn't grow my little startup into a top 20 Web Host and Domain Business. Like so many other dotcoms back in the day, Web.com started in the basement. We had a little money, a few computers, and no idea how to run a business.

We worked incredibly hard, got lucky more often than not, and we brought every bit of talent, passion, commitment and intensity we had to the task. And it worked! In the first couple of years, we learned about service delivery and customer service. We invented web hosting and domain registration technologies that had never existed before. We learned how to take great care of our customers. We were on our way!

In our third year, we broke the code for online marketing. We absolutely nailed it. Turning our advertising dollars into clients and customers grew into one of our greatest strengths. Some said we were better at online marketing than we were at web hosting, and that was our core business! The team was growing, and we were making money, and living the dotcom dream. What could possibly go wrong?

And that's when we hit the wall. One day our wildest growth dreams were coming true, and the next we were being crushed by our own success. We would get a thousand new customers from our amazing marketing, but we would lose eleven hundred because we couldn't keep up with customer service demands. We couldn't hire enough people to run the business properly, and we for-all into a purpose-driven team where everything important to success was measured, and we were all accountable to one another.

At first, nobody - and I mean nobody - liked it. Some teammates (we stopped calling them employees) did not want to be held accountable. They did not want to set monthly goals or take ownership of their problems. In a way, I didn't blame them. It was different. A one hundred eighty turn from how things used to be. We lost some people because they just couldn't adapt. There were times I wanted to give up as well.

But after a while, our system started to take hold. We were achieving measurable, consistent results. We were setting goals, and hitting them most of the time. Entire departments started using the system. Managers learned to coach their employees, not just tell them what to do. Stress went down, customer retention went up. Productivity was increasing. Profits went up, expenses went down. Before you knew it, we were a Top 20 Domain and Hosting company worldwide. It. Was. Incredible.

Then it hit me! It was not my fault that the business had been eating itself alive. It was not my fault that I had been in reactive mode all the time. It was not my fault that there weren't enough hours in a day to take care of my employees and customers at the rate we were growing. Truth be told, it was actually my talent and my passion for the business that helped us get as far as we did. All these things were definitely my problems. But they were not my fault.

There was something else going on in the background, and I cannot believe it took me so long to figure it out. I know now that before I had this insight I never stood a chance. Business problems are like quicksand. The more you struggle the faster you sink! Nobody ever told me that. As a matter of fact, there were a lot of things that nobody told me.

The thing that kept me from achieving success, from breaking through to the next level, was what I call old-school thinking and naysayers. People who said I was not cut out for business, or did not have the education, or the talent to make it. Employees and partners who were all too willing to accept failure, instead of digging in and growing beyond who and what we were at the time. People who would rather fix the blame than fix the problem.

Naysayers and old school thinkers. Whenever something went well, they would tell me I was lucky. Whenever I hit a bump in the road they would say, "I told you so! You are not up to this!" Certain people were great at making excuses, and awful at solving problems.

It was Jim Rohn who said, "You are the average of the five people you spend the most time with." Think about it. The people I spent the most time with were overwhelmed, overworked teammates, concerned and sometimes angry customers, and friends with 'real' jobs who were all just waiting for me to grow up. They all cared for me and they all meant well. But at the same time, they were holding me back. Pulling me down.

If you're struggling like I was, chances are it is not your fault either. Chances are, you have got all the ingredients you need for a successful business. You just need to combine those ingredients differently. Stop using the same old recipe that never worked. As soon as you make that move, you are in for an amazing adventure. I know because that is exactly what I did.

After we got our leadership system in place, the business took off like never before. When team leaders actually started communicating with one another, we could dial up our amazing marketing, knowing that the customer service team would be ready to take on the extra work. We started to measure performance and recognize great contributions across the whole company. Our new leadership system took off and we never looked back!

The biggest surprise of all came when I realized that the system didn't just work for me and my business. It could work for any business. Any business at all.

Who's the Leader?

The second question that you should ask as a member of a team is, "Who's the leader?" When nobody is in charge, everybody is in charge. Achieving goals requires action. Taking action requires a plan. Having a plan requires an understanding of the big picture, and breaking that understanding down into action steps. The success of a team depends upon coordinated effort. When there is more than one way to get something done, and there always is, choices must be made. When two or more teammates disagree on the best course of action, someone needs to make the final decision. That someone is the leader. Without a clearly defined leader there is a significantly reduced chance for success.

At the most basic level leaders settle disputes. The leader keeps everyone moving in the same direction. Leaders also set the tone for a team. They convey the vision and help the team understand why the goals are important. Leaders inspire and motivate us. Effective leaders bring out the best in their

teammates. When you think about a successful organization or a high performing team, chances are you will start thinking about their leader. Tesla, for example. If you say Tesla, I think of Elon Musk. His vision, passion, drive, decision-making and guidance have helped Tesla defy the odds to become the premier manufacturer of electric cars. There is no question about who leads Tesla. Organizations without clarity about who the leader is are destined to obscurity or failure. You should always know what's the goal and who's the leader!

Exercise: What's the Goal?

Write your goal for reading this book in the space below.

By the time I finish reading this book, I will

_____

_____

_____

_____

_____

_____

_____

_____

_____

_____

_____

_____ .

Two Musts for Every Meeting

arvard Business Review reports that sixty five percent of senior managers surveyed feel that meetings keep them from completing their own work. Seventy one percent said meetings are unproductive and inefficient. Sixty four percent said meetings come at the expense of deep thinking. Sixty two percent said meetings miss opportunities to bring the team closer together.

Employees report that more than thirty percent of their time is spent in unproductive meetings. Thirty percent! More than one day a week of every business week is perceived as wasted time.

Winning teams and successful organizations have as much as thirty percent more productive time because they waste less time in meetings. Winning organizations do meetings right, and average or subpar organizations don't. Since running an effective, time-saving meeting is a major differentiator between winners and losers, you might be asking yourself, "How do we run effective, time-saving meetings?" Let's sort that out right now.

You are less than one chapter away from ever having to suffer – or cause others to suffer – a bad meeting!

A Shared Agenda

Two things are required for a meeting to be a meeting. Most of us know the first one. In live Goal Boss Workshops, we ask for a whole list of suggestions and the very first thing participants will call out will be, of course, an agenda! This is absolutely true. A meeting is not a meeting if there's no written, shared agenda. Without an agenda, it is just a get together.

Why must we have an agenda in order for a meeting to be a meeting? To answer that question, think back to one of your recent meetings, which you may recall as more of a freeform conversation than a focused discussion about particular issues. Exploratory conversations can be interesting, engaging, and fulfilling. They are always great at parties and awful in meetings. Even brainstorming sessions or ideation meetings are more productive and effective with an agenda. We will get into why that is so, and how you can leverage the immense creativity of your team.

Perhaps the most efficient thing about an agenda is that it sets the times and the topics for your meeting. With a written and shared agenda, you will always know what you are going to talk about during that meeting. Everyone involved will know what the goals are for the meeting. Everyone will know when the meeting is scheduled to start and best of all everyone in the room will know when the meeting is scheduled to end. Time is the only thing you cannot get more of. We all know this instinctively. We also know that no one trusts a thief. If you steal time from people by extending meetings, your team will trust you less. It is that simple. Do not waste one minute that you don't have to. Don't. Steal. Time!

Remember that the people you have invited to your meeting cannot get any more time either. That is why we want to be extremely respectful of time. The first step in respecting your time, that of others and managing time overall is to provide an agenda for your meetings. A simple agenda lets everyone involved know what you are going to discuss during the meeting, what the goals are for the meeting, when it will start, and when it will end. Certainty is a beautiful thing.

Speaking of certainty, you might notice that the Table of Contents in this book is our agenda. We are going to discuss and learn about leadership strategies, teamwork and accountability, Key Metrics, Goals, and Team Problem Solving. These are the building blocks of the Goal Boss Leadership System. You will learn how to facilitate Goal Boss Meetings and that will help you and your team get more done. It will help you and your team foster a culture of high performance and drive results. You will learn specific skills of communication, planning, organizing, controlling, leading. These are the Five Keys to Leadership.

You will learn about Rapid Values Onboarding and employee engagement because finding and keeping the right people in your organization is another differentiator between winners and also-rans. We will look at how to get - and give - the best results for and with your teammates through effective coaching. The goal of this book is to give you the tools, strategies and techniques you need to grow a successful organization.

Ground Rules

What is the second thing we need for a meeting to be a meeting? Say you're on a business trip and you go to the pool at the hotel. When you enter the swimming pool area, you will probably see a sign on the gate with things like: "No lifeguard on duty. No glass containers. Pool closes at 10 p.m." A quick list of rules. Why? The thing about a hotel swimming pool at a hotel, or any other purpose-built environment, is that those environments always have rules. The swimming pool rules exist to keep people safe, comfortable, and to make sure you get what you came for when you go to the pool. I am talking about meeting Ground Rules. You will find Ground Rules exist in every specialized environment. Swimming pools, your gym, the airport, amusement parks, hospitals, factories, and so on. The more important the facility, the easier it will be to know the ground rules. Is your business important? Is your meeting important?

Ground Rules are critical to any business undertaking. A meeting or conference room is a purpose-built environment. Important things happen there. The conference room is where big decisions are made. Good ones and bad ones. People can get hurt in a conference room. Careers can be ended, customers can be lost, trust can be eroded, leadership can fail. To conduct business as though your conference room is not a potentially dangerous environment is naive. Perhaps I am overstating things to make a point. If I am, I am not overstating it by much.

We need ground rules so you know what to expect from me, and I know what to expect from you. We need ground rules so we all understand where the boundaries are. We need ground rules so we know what is and is not expected of us. Ground rules are absolutely crucial. Goal Boss clients have the ground rules posted on the wall in their conference rooms. When anybody enters the environment, they can see what the rules are that will permit them to get the most out of the experience. Below are the standard ground rules we use at Goal Boss. These should serve as a great starting point for you and your conference room in your business.

Confidentiality

We protect your information very carefully. If you share something with us, we are not going to share it with somebody else without your express permission. Confidentiality is absolutely crucial because it creates what is called psychological safety. If I know that I can say something in this environment and it won't be repeated outside of the environment, then I feel safe and I'm able to discuss things that are important.

Teamwork

We work together as a team. Individuals go fast, but teams go far. Along with teamwork comes accountability. If I make a promise to my team, I am going to come through. It is important that we take those promises seriously.

Everyone Participates

We need everyone in the meeting to participate. Even the quiet ones. So, we have developed tools and techniques we use to get people to come out of their shells a little bit, participate and contribute to the team. The quiet ones are usually the well-informed ones, too. We need to make sure that the quiet ones get in the game and stay there.

No Sidebars

Few things are more disruptive to a high performing team than the sidebar. A sidebar is when two or more people in a meeting start a quiet conversation of their own while someone else in the meeting is talking. Sidebars obliterate teamwork. At the most obvious level, a sidebar shows disregard for the person talking, and for the group as a whole. Just as important is the fact that when two people are having their own private meeting within the meeting, the rest of the team can no longer rely on or benefit from their contribution. Keeping focus on your team, especially when the conversation may not directly involve you, is a hallmark of high performance and teamwork. So, no sidebars.

Airplane Mode

In terms of passive meeting disruption, smartphones, tablets, laptops and mobile electronics run close on the heels of sidebars when it comes to eroding teamwork and productivity. If you have time to process email or do other work while you are in a meeting, it is a sure sign that your meeting is a waste of time. Or at the very least, you are not needed there. Turn off your phone. Be present in the room for your teammates and your organization.

Candid, Timely Feedback

A lot of times in a meeting, if somebody says something you disagree with, you might let it slide just because you don't want to make people uncomfortable. You don't want to make waves. You don't want to rock the boat. Sometimes, you just don't want to make the meeting last any longer than it has to! Candid, timely feedback is one of our ground rules. It is one of the ground rules in Goal Boss Meetings and Goal Boss Coaching. If you do not understand or agree with a point being made, speak up! Ask questions. Be prepared to give - and receive - candid, timely feedback.

Manage Time. Ruthlessly

Time is the only thing you cannot get more of. So, we manage time ruthlessly. Meetings - and exercises within those meetings - start on time. Just as important is the fact that meetings end on time. Don't take hostages!

No Rabbit Holes

Huge amounts of time get wasted in meetings every day on trivial conversations. Most of us are curious. Most of us love a good story. Some of us like to distract from what is really important. By using a code word like, "Rabbit Hole," we can quickly and politely get the team back on track when the team begins to wander.

Attack the Problem, Not the Person

If you find an issue with a teammate, or your boss, or your organization, or even a client- you must make sure that everyone knows that it is the problem you are going after, not the person. Imagine starting a conversation by saying, "I noticed your numbers are off a little bit. What can we do to get that back on track?" That is what attacking the problem looks like.

Now, imagine starting that same conversation with "What's wrong with you? Why are your numbers so bad?" Now, it is personal. Attacking the person makes it harder to get to the problem. Once you have attacked the person, you have to repair the relationship before you can address the problem. It rarely helps to start off with an attack. So, attack the problem, not the person. We never attack the person.

Important Things Can't Be Discussed Comfortably

Think about the last time you were at the gym. If you were doing it right, you were achy, you were tired, you were out of breath, you were working hard. It is not comfortable to be at the gym if you're doing it right. No one expects to be comfortable at the gym. In business meetings, it is also okay to be uncomfortable because that is where the important things are being addressed. Discomfort is not a reason to avoid important topics. Letting people know this in advance helps your team step up their game.

In terms of ground rules, those are the basics and they will work for just about any meeting. If you haven't created your very own custom ground rules yet, start with these. I promise they will work far better than no ground rules at all. Your ground rules can be changed to suit your situation, your particular organization, or the needs of your team. The ground rules for this book have been set and we are going to stick to them. It really is important.

When you bring an Agenda and Ground Rules to your meeting, you will get more done, you will build teamwork, and you will transform your organization into a high performing team.

Key Takeaways

In the space below, write your Key Takeaways from this chapter.

_____

_____

_____

_____

_____

_____

_____

_____

_____

_____

_____

_____

_____

_____

GROUND RULES

- Confidentiality
- Teamwork
- Everyone Participates
- No Sidebars
- Airplane Mode
- Candid, Timely Feedback
- Manage Time. Ruthlessly
- No Rabbit Holes
- Attack the Problem, Not the Person
- Important Things Can't Be Discussed Comfortably

goal boss

CHAPTER THREE

The Goal Boss Process

The Goal Boss Process can provide a roadmap for you to develop the leadership skills you need to transform yourself into a high performing member of a high performing team. It will show you how to get more done in your organization than you ever thought possible. The Goal Boss Leadership System is designed to offer you multiple opportunities and tools to help you look at yourself objectively as a leader. Introspection is a potent aspect of being a leader. You cannot be an effective leader unless you are always willing to look at yourself, sometimes in unflattering ways.

Leaders must step up and accept the things about themselves that need to improve. If you gloss over your weaknesses, or try to ignore them completely, you are going to be spinning your wheels and you will not go as far as you want to.

We share all of the tools, strategies and techniques we teach in our signature Goal Boss Workshop. There are a few interactive differences to keep in mind since this is a book, and not a live workshop. As you read, there won't be a Goal Boss Certified Coach in the room to work with you. However, understanding the process of our live training and what our participants learn and take away from those events can help you create your personal strategy designed to achieve the same results in a self-study environment.

Your journey starts with our ten-question self-assessment which appears below. Be honest! Be straightforward about your strengths and opportunities for improvement in the questionnaire.

Throughout the course of the book, you will learn how to use the Goal Boss Leadership System. I encourage you to set two short term business goals; those are goals that you are going to accomplish in the next thirty or forty-five days. You should also create two long-term business goals that you are going to accomplish in the next twelve months. Finally, you will set two professional development goals. Professional development goals are about you, the ways that you can improve yourself. In general, the beneficiary of your business goals will be your organization. Your professional development goals are about you. They are about improving your personal leadership skills. If you move to another organization someday, you will take that professional development with you.

If you decide to use the Goal Boss Platform, all that information will be in your very own Goal Boss account. It is a fact that you are ten times more likely to achieve a goal if you write it down. Goal Boss is purpose built to help you achieve your goals. This is your opportunity to master goal setting.

When you bought this book, you received an invitation to use the Goal Boss Platform, attend our webinars, trainings and events - many of which are complimentary. As an owner of this book, you will have an exclusive opportunity to take advantage of our webinars where we get together with people who know Goal Boss. You will be able to share your short-term and long-term goals, get feedback from peers, and report on the action steps you have started to take to move your business in the right direction.

You will soon discover that you are not alone. There are valuable resources and people available to advise and encourage you along the way. As you become part of this tribe, part of the Goal Boss community, you are going to be more successful. You are going to develop superior leadership skills.

Success is a process, not an event. There is no light switch that we can flip to just instantly make you successful. Anybody who tells you that is about to ask you for your credit card number. Amazing accomplishments happen a little bit at a time, over time. So, we are going to follow up and follow up and follow up and we will be here for you as long as you want. We are ready to put in the work. Are you?

Self-Assessment

Here is your Goal Boss Self-Assessment. Don't flinch! Looking at yourself objectively and honestly is a core quality of an effective leader. Successful people do this. So, do this!

What are your strengths as a leader?

_____

_____

_____

_____

In what areas of leadership and management would you like to see yourself improve the most?

_____

_____

_____

_____

_____

_____

What are your career goals for the next three months?

_____

_____

_____

_____

_____

_____

What are your career goals for the next twelve months?

_____

_____

_____

_____

_____

_____

When communicating with others, what are your biggest concerns? How could you improve?

_____

_____

_____

_____

_____

_____

When it comes to planning, how are you at setting clear goals, making a plan and managing projects?

_____

_____

_____

_____

_____

_____

When it comes to organizing resources like time, people and money, where do you struggle the most?

_____

_____

_____

_____

_____

_____

What are your biggest challenges regarding accountability, measuring performance, implementing corrective measures, and driving results?

_____

_____

_____

_____

_____

_____

What are your biggest challenges in motivation, building consensus, teamwork and inspiring others to take action?

_____

_____

_____

_____

_____

_____

What is holding you back from overcoming your challenges and achieving your goals?

_____

_____

_____

_____

Goal Boss 360

The live Goal Boss Process includes a facilitated three hundred sixty-degree review of your strengths and opportunities for improvement. The Goal Boss 360 starts by having you nominate between five and ten people who know you best. Co-workers, partners, employees, friends, and even your customers are all great sources for this kind of feedback. The Goal Boss Platform then sends a confidential questionnaire to your "Goal Boss 360 Team." Before the workshop starts, a Goal Boss Certified Coach will personally analyze that feedback to learn about your leadership style before you ever get to the workshop. We customize the Goal Boss Workshop experience for every single participant. Goal Boss Certified Coaches are trained to analyze this feedback, and to present information to you in a positive, productive matter. When it comes to 360 Feedback, we strongly suggest that you don't try this at home.

Key Takeaways

In the space below, write your Key Takeaways from this chapter.

_____

_____

_____

_____

_____

_____

_____

_____

_____

_____

_____

_____

_____

_____

_____

_____

CHAPTER FOUR

The Goal Boss System

The Goal Boss Leadership System gets results and provides immediate, measurable return on investment. Goal Boss is built on three main concepts, or pillars. For now, let's dip our toes in the water, so to speak, with a quick look the three pillars of Goal Boss. We'll dig deeper later.

Key Metrics

The first pillar of the Goal Boss Platform is Key Metrics. Key Metrics are the things in your business, in your life and in your organization, that really matter. We rarely have a hard time understanding the concept of Key Metrics. The things that matter most are, by definition, key. Dig any deeper than that, and you might find it is not so easy to give names to those things. How do we figure out what our Key Metrics are? We have developed a simple, almost comically easy way to do just that.

To identify your Key Metrics, make a list of the 10 things that you are most proud of and the 10 things that you are most worried about. It is that simple. There is no faster way to figure out what matters most. By making your Two Top Ten lists, you can come up with the Key Metrics of your business, or of your life. Make the Two Top Ten lists with your team, and you will have the Key Metrics for your entire organization.

Key Metrics are the things that we think about the most. The things that really make a difference. In later chapters, we will go into Key Metrics in more detail, how they figure into the Goal Boss Platform, and what you can do to control them.

Goals

The second pillar of Goal Boss is Goals. Once we've identified our Key Metrics, the next step is to set goals. We want to set goals that are going to move the needle on our Key Metrics. Be certain you set goals designed to increase revenue, decrease inefficiency or cost, increase closed deals, and so forth. Goal Boss allows you to control your Key Metrics through a simple, effective system of setting, measuring and achieving goals. More on that in chapters to come!

Team Problem Solving

Because into every life a little rain must fall, the third pillar of the Goal Boss Platform is our problem-solving methodology called Team Problem Solving. TPS for short. Team Problem Solving is based on how the folks at NASA work things out.

We use a rocket scientist process to solve problems on our Goal Boss Teams and even when we are working on things one-on-one or by ourselves. The key takeaway for now about Team Problem Solving is that it is a proven way to leverage the best thinking of your team to discuss problems, determine action steps to resolve those problems, and establish points of accountability to ensure you do not keep covering the same ground over and over again. A business cycle is too short to deal with the same problems over and over again.

The Goal Boss System helps you assign value to what matters to you through Key Metrics. It provides a framework to set and achieve meaningful goals. When you run into trouble, Goal Boss Team Problem Solving helps you dismantle the barriers preventing you from moving the needle on the Key Metrics. Key Metrics, Goals, Team Problem Solving. Rinse, and repeat.

Key Takeaways

In the space below, write your Key Takeaways from this chapter.

_____

_____

_____

_____

_____

_____

_____

_____

_____

_____

_____

_____

_____

_____

CHAPTER FIVE

The Five Principles of Goal Boss

The five principles of Goal Boss are the rock on which our house is built. These are the values we strive to exemplify in every single thing we do. They are teamwork, hard work, communication, delegation and time management.

Teamwork

The first principle of the Goal Boss system is teamwork. An individual can go fast, but a team can go far. One of the reasons we use this rowing metaphor so much is because rowing is all about teamwork. Crew is the oldest sport in the United States. It is also one of the hardest, the most technical, the most complicated and the least visible. Crew is not flashy. When it is done well it looks easy and effortless. There are no rock stars in this sport. There is no one person who makes the whole thing happen. Crew is totally reliant on team. That is why they call it "crew!" The actual personal goal in rowing is to not be the best rower in the boat, but to make sure that your boat is the best boat. Think about that for a minute!

Teamwork is critically important. Using the Goal Boss Leadership System, we value the team over the individual because we know that teams go far. We know that personal satisfaction comes along with helping others and contributing to the goal. That is why the principle of teamwork is one of our core values.

Hard Work

Let's do a thought experiment. You take all the smart people for your team and I'll take all the hard-working people for mine. Then we'll have a competition. You may pick the competition. Whatever you want it to be. Eight times out of ten, my hard-working team will beat your smart team. Why? Because hard work works most of the time. Hard workers bring determination and grit to every task they take on. Hard workers are prepared for the fact that things don't always come easily.

Smart people, on the other hand, often get used to things coming easily. And why not? they are smart. A highly intelligent child, for example, will breeze through elementary school and middle school with little difficulty. They test successfully, they understand the material. Incredibly smart kids can even glide through high school without breaking a sweat. Then comes college.

Just about everyone attending college is smart. In college being smart is not a differentiator. High intelligence does not set you apart from peers in college. If you are unaccustomed to hard work when this happens, you will struggle at best, and fail completely at worst. Meanwhile, the not-so-smart kid who had to work hard for every good grade they ever got, is unsurprised when they get to college. They have always worked hard and they don't expect anything different in college.

Think for a moment about the most successful people you know personally. Think for a moment about your boss, or the CEO of your company. Are they the smartest people you have ever met? Are they smarter than you? Maybe. The boss is not always the smartest person in the organization. Usually, however, he is one of the hardest workers.

Hard work is one of the principles on which Goal Boss is built. We value hard work. We have succeeded. I have succeeded not because I have always been the smartest, not because I have always had the best idea, and not because I was always first to market with a product or a service. I succeed because I make it my business to work harder than anybody else.

Communication

Communication is the third principle of Goal Boss, and number three in our list of core values. Communication is a skill we must continue developing as we grow. There is no end to the work on communication. The definition of communicating is to get someone to understand your thoughts, ideas, or feelings. This skill can be developed into a leadership superpower.

The ability to get others to actually understand your thoughts, ideas, or feelings, and to clearly understand the thoughts, ideas, or feelings of others can unlock unlimited potential. When you struggle to make yourself understood your leadership suffers, and your career will stall. Effective leaders are always developing their communication skills.

The good news about communicating is that it is a skill, not a gift You do not need to be a natural born communicator in order to become an expert at communicating. I have yet to meet someone who cannot improve their communication skills. Like everything in the Goal Boss Leadership System, communicating is simple. The tools for becoming an expert communicator are in this book.

Delegation

Getting things done without doing everything yourself is a critical aspect of growing as a leader and growing your organization. You cannot lead a successful company without learning to delegate. You cannot make vice president or CEO without learning to delegate. As you pass through the stages of leadership, your delegation skills will have to improve and then improve and then improve some more. We will get into the mechanics of delegation later when we teach you exactly how to delegate like an expert. Delegation is one of our five principles because when you empower someone to do something, particularly something important, you have more time to do things that only you can do.

Delegating is both a science and an art form. Along with communication and time management, delegation is one of the Big Three Career Killers. Put another way, when you reach the limit of your delegation skills, when you are not able to delegate complicated tasks to others, that is where your career may falter. To grow as a leader, you must continue to get more and more tasks done without doing those things yourself.

Ask yourself if there is anyone else who can do the task you are about to start. If so, delegate! Only do what only you can do!

Time Management

Time is the only thing you can't get more of. Sooner or later, we all run out of time. Sadly, time is also one of the resources people squander the most.

Time management is one of the principles of Goal Boss because there is nothing more valuable than time. It is the only thing you can't get more of. If you don't manage time, time will manage you. As you learn to use the Goal Boss Leadership System and leverage these tools, strategies and techniques for getting stuff done, you will develop your time management skills. Time Management is one of the Big Three Career Killers. If you are not an expert at managing time, you will end up working for someone who is.

Key Takeaways

In the space below, write your Key Takeaways from this chapter.

_____

_____

_____

_____

_____

_____

_____

_____

_____

_____

_____

_____

_____

CHAPTER SIX

Key Metrics

Vilfredo Pareto, an Italian economist, discovered that eighty percent of the land in Italy was owned by twenty percent of the people. This spurred his curiosity. Pareto wanted to know if this was a political issue, or a universal issue. Was this politics, was it human behavior, or was it science? To answer this question, Pareto took to his garden. Being a botanist, among other things, it made perfect sense to study the peas in his garden. Pareto discovered that eighty percent of the peas grew from twenty percent of the peapods.

Throughout his life, Pareto studied many different systems and situations. His work confirmed time and again that what we now know as the Eighty-Twenty Rule applies to nearly every system you can name. The Eighty-Twenty Rule is a natural phenomenon. It is how the world works. Everything from the peas in Pareto's garden to the bugs in a software product follow this rule. Eighty percent of your revenue comes from twenty percent of your products. Eighty percent of your customer service problems are going to come from twenty percent of your customers. According to Microsoft, eighty percent of their customer complaints come from twenty percent of the bugs. The Eighty-Twenty Rule is demonstrated over and over again.

> ### *Eighty-Twenty Rule Key Takeaways*
>
> *80% of the work is completed by 20% of your team (I'm going to help you improve this)*
>
> *80% of software problems are caused by 20% of the software bugs (software companies are painfully aware of this fact)*
>
> *80% of customers use 20% of the software features (when was the last time you used the Cross-Reference function inside Microsoft Word?)*
>
> *80% of sales come from 20% of your sales people*

Pareto's twenty percent that he called the precious few, is where you find the motor for peak performance. The details that make big differences. We call these the Key Metrics - the things that matter most.

Focus makes the difference between an average business and a high-performing business. Identifying and understanding the Key Metrics of your business is vitally important to your success. Key Metrics are the things that matter most. The twenty percent of your work that yields eighty percent of your results.

By adopting the Goal Boss Leadership System, you will focus yourself and your team on the things that drive your business, and to set goals and take actions to improve those things. The process is so straightforward that many cannot believe it will work. But it does. Key Metrics are a fundamental part of the Goal Boss Leadership System. Key Metrics are the twenty percent of your actions that yield eighty percent of your results. Key Metrics are how you leverage Pareto's Eighty-Twenty Rule.

Anyone attempting to develop a high performing organization needs to understand Key Metrics and how they apply. There are five points to define in preparation for measuring the Key Metrics of your business in a way that will effectively foster teamwork and leadership in your organization. Name, category, owner, data type and variance type.

Categories

It is necessary to identify and categorize the Key Metrics of your business to help you and your teammates determine what actions can be taken to improve performance in a particular area. Key Metrics fall into four categories. Profit and loss, productivity, quality, or cash flow.

Profit & Loss

Key Metrics in the profit and loss category describe the financials and accounting of the business. This includes revenue, gross profit, sales, new customers, overhead expense, labor cost, orders booked, average revenue per unit, etc. Key Metrics from other categories usually roll up to profit and loss.

Productivity

Key Metrics in the productivity category measure how much is getting done at the operations level of an organization. They are quantitative measurements that describe how well the business is doing what it does. Examples of Key Metrics that show the details of productivity might be labor cost, employee turnover, closing percentage, safety, average wait time, advertising conversion rates, on-time delivery rate, etc.

Quality

Key Metrics in the quality category measure how smooth and accurate the business process is. Details in this category may include customer satisfaction, repeat business, warranty repairs, product returns, net promoter score, quality assurance, etc.

Cash Flow

Key Metrics in the cash flow category are just that. It is one of the easiest to measure, and sometimes among the hardest to improve. Examples of cash flow Key Metrics are accounts receivable, cash on hand, inventory turns, aging, shrinkage, and available credit.

Ownership

Each Key Metric in your business must be assigned an owner. One owner. For each Key Metric, one person is responsible for measuring performance of that Key Metric as well as determining what actions may be taken to make sure that performance is positive. The owner assumes the primary leadership position with regard to the performance of their Key Metric. Each owner is not necessarily the only person doing all of the work involved in keeping their Key Metrics moving in the right direction. We have teams!

Data Type

Key Metrics are measured in one of three ways. Dollars, Percentage, Numbers. Making this determination when you set up your Key Metrics ensures the whole team will understand how and where a particular Key Metric impacts the business.

Variance Type

When a Key Metric varies from month to month, it is either good or not so good. Variance type answers the simple question of whether more is better or less is better. The Key Metric of sales will have a variance type of More is Better simply because more sales is indeed better. On the other hand, call center wait times for the customer support department would be measured with a Less is Better variance type.

When you define each of these five points for the Key Metrics of your business, you vastly simplify reporting on performance. This saves valuable time in meetings, because when you present performance data in these categories, the need to understand the detailed workings of every part of the business is significantly reduced or even eliminated. Only the Key Metric owner needs to understand the deep details. The rest of the team will have just the level of information required to see how the other parts of the business are performing. Key Metrics reporting is presented in monthly Goal Boss Meetings. First focus on setting up your Key Metrics.

The Goal Boss Platform was built in my never-ending search for the twenty percent of everything that gets us eighty percent of our results. My goal is to give you the twenty percent that matters most. To give you the most potent, most effective, most powerful tools that you can use in business.

Exercise: On a sheet of paper write down at least three Key Metrics for your business. For each Key Metric, be sure to include:

Key Metric Name

Category

Owner

Data Type

Variance Type

TIP: If you prefer, you can enter all this information into the Goal Boss app which was built specifically for this purpose. It's free, and the app will keep track of everything for you. How you get it done is up to you. The important thing is to do it!

Identify the things that matter most. At the end of every chapter and every topic, write down your key takeaways. What are the things that apply most to you and your business from what you just read? In our workshops, both live and online, we quiz you along the way to make sure that you are getting the main points. What you find important is what matters the most. It is what you decide to implement that will provide your results.

Key Takeaways

In the space below, write your Key Takeaways from this chapter.

_____

_____

_____

_____

_____

_____

_____

_____

_____

_____

_____

_____

_____

_____

CHAPTER SEVEN

Behave Yourself!

No two people are alike. We have different ideas, experience, knowledge, talents and values. Different people enjoy different activities. How our differences come across, and how we use these differences as strengths is a matter of style. Specifically, behavioral style. The personality test known as DISC has been a game changer for millions of people.

There are four major behavioral styles: Dominance, Influence, Steadiness, and Compliance. Happily, great minds have been hard at work on the issue of behavioral style for the better part of a century.

In 1921, Swiss psychiatrist and psychoanalyst Carl Jung identified four dominant impulses that guide behavior in his book <u>Psychological Types</u>. These four impulses are Intuition, Feeling, Thinking, and Sensation.

In 1928, William Moulton Marston, Ph.D. identified four dominant personality traits that guide behavior in his book <u>The</u>

<u>Emotions of Normal People at Harvard</u>. These four traits are Dominance, Influence, Steadiness, and Compliance.

1940, the first DISC survey was produced by Walter Clark, based on Marston's theories and research. The assessment focuses on the same four personality traits as Marston identified, resulting in a highly accurate measurement of these traits, called Behavioral Style. The Behavioral Style of an individual can change based on one's environment at work, at home, or socially.

The Four DISC Styles

Dominance - *Dominant, Decisive, Direct, Goal-Oriented*

Influence - *Influential, Outgoing, Optimistic, Enthusiastic*

Steadiness - *Steady, Sympathetic, Patient, Good-Listeners*

Compliance - *Compliant, Conscientious, Organized, Creative*

Thanks to Jung, Marston, Clark, and other researchers and practitioners who followed, we can use DISC to predict and manage communication, teamwork, productivity for ourselves and the people we rely on. Each of us has a particular, identifiable, and predictable way of dealing with situations, opportunities, information and people. Because of your behavioral style, you will respond more or less favorably to certain words or situations.

Understanding these principles is a superpower. DISC opens the door to better managing your time and your communication with others. It allows you to predict and make sense of why you are so good at some things, and maybe not so good at others. DISC is a powerful tool that you can begin to use today. Your ability to communicate your needs, your ability to engage and motivate others to help you, or to help themselves, is vastly important to how your business will operate, both inside and out. Your behavioral style determines the kinds of things you are likely to be good at - or enjoy - and the kinds of things you probably won't be very good at, and wouldn't enjoy. If you understand the roles in your business that you are behaviorally suited for, you can concentrate on performing those roles and figure out ways to leverage the rest.

Each of us has a particular, identifiable, and somewhat predictable way of dealing with situations, opportunities, information and people. Depending on what your personal behavioral style is, you respond more favorably to certain words or situations, and less favorably to others. It's important to understand how this works. Understanding these principles opens the door to better managing your time and your communication with others. Your ability to communicate wants and needs, and your ability to engage, enroll and motivate others to help you, or to help themselves, can significantly increase the quality of your life, your business, your relationships. DISC is a proven system for doing just that.

When you know how to understand the style of the person you are talking to, the chances of working well with them increase significantly.

We are going to get further into the details of behavioral style and DISC and you can become a master of communication when you begin to understand behavioral style.

Dominance, influence, steadiness, compliance. The acronym we use is DISC. We talk a lot about DISC in Goal Boss because

DISC assessments and DISC are a fast way for you and your team to become experts in communicating, problem solving, accomplishing your goals.

Dominance

You recognize a dominant person when you meet them. They are strong-willed, ambitious, decisive, and competitive. They like to be in charge. When a dominant person walks in the room, they want everybody to do what they say, or there is going to be some kind of tension. In terms of behavioral style, we call this person a "High D." We all know the dominant, or High-D behavioral style when we encounter it. We will often, but not always, find High D people in leadership roles like CEO, director, and manager. Direct and forceful, they value achievement, are fast-paced and task oriented.

A list of High D personalities from fact and fiction would include

> Arnold Schwarzenegger (actor/politician)
> Cher (musician)
> Darth Vader (fictional character)
> Gordon Ramsay (television personality)
> James T. Kirk (fictional character)
> Simon Cowell (television personality)
> Tiger Woods (athlete)

Influence

The next behavioral style is the influence style. Influence-oriented people, or "High I" people, want you to subscribe to their belief systems. They want you to see things their way, to look at the world through their eyes. They are charismatic, enthusiastic, convincing, and sociable. They are the life of the party. They plan the party! Influence oriented people want everybody to get along. If you are a "High I" person, you already know what I'm talking about. If you are not influence-oriented, you probably wonder why that would be so important. Influence oriented people fit naturally into roles in sales, public relations, and politics. They know how to "read a room," and "give people what they want".

Here are a few examples of High I personalities from fact and fiction.

> Andre Agassi (athlete)
> Bill Clinton (former President of the United States)
> Eddie Murphy (actor)
> Han Solo (fictional character)
> Oprah Winfrey (TV host)

Steadiness

Steadiness people value continuity. "High S" people tend to drive the same way to work every day. Steadiness people are low-key. They need time to warm up to an idea. "High S" people come across as relaxed. They are patient and deliberate. They are consistent. Steadiness people move through work, and life, deliberately and carefully. They like to start at the beginning, work through the middle and keep going until the end. They don't like to jump into things the way a "High D" person would. "High S" folks are not as concerned about getting everybody to feel and think the way they do. Steadiness people like a methodical pace. They like to take their time and get it right. "High S" people are well suited to supportive roles like therapist or human resources manager. A few notable "High S" personalities from fact and fiction would include:

> Jimmy Carter (former President of the United States)
> Luke Skywalker (fictional character)
> Mahatma Gandhi (civil rights leader)
> Mother Teresa (religious figure)
> Ted Danson (actor)

Compliance

Last, but not least, is the compliance oriented person. The "High C". Compliance people are rule followers. They value the rules. they are cautious and tactful, accurate, systematic, and they love the details. You will often find compliance oriented people in finance organizations or in finance parts of the organization. They are the Chief Financial Officer, the accountant, the bookkeeper, or the safety officer. "High C's" can get deep into the details. They do not like to cut corners and they do not like easy answers. Examples of "High C" style from fact and fiction would include:

Albert Einstein (physicist)
Bill Gates (businessman)
C-3PO (fictional character)
Henry Kissinger (politician)
Kevin Costner (actor)

DISC Roles

Various combinations of styles result in different individuals being best suited to particular roles.

Dominance and influence oriented people tend to be shapers of the environment. Dominance people want everybody to line up and do what they say. Influence oriented people want everybody to show up and participate. High D's and High I's are the people are out there changing the world.

Compliance and steadiness oriented people are more apt to be managers of the environment. They make sure that after the influence oriented person rearranges all the chairs at the party, that the chairs stay the way they should be. Compliance and steadiness people make sure that the environment is usable but they don't change it very much. High C and High S people are probably not going to break the rules and develop a new business process. But without them there would be no one to fine tune all the new innovations our High D rule breakers build, or to support the new products the High I is out there selling. High S and High C folks manage the environment.

Compliance and dominance people are usually task-oriented. A compliance oriented person and a dominance oriented person will make sure that they and the people they work with are executing the tasks that fit the environment. A dominance oriented person will expect you to follow their lead, build what they design. A compliance oriented person wants you to observe the rules, fill out the form, follow the process. Our High C and High D teammates are happy and engaged when there are tasks in play.

Steadiness and influence oriented people, the High-S and the High-I folks, are all about people. An influence oriented person wants to know how you feel. They value empathy. A steadiness oriented person is going to listen to your ideas, thoughts, feelings, hopes, dreams, fears and concerns. The High S won't empathize quite as much as the High I but they will listen to you. High S and High I are the people-oriented behavioral styles. An influence oriented person could fit well into role of public relations. A steadiness oriented person could fit well into a role of counselor, human resources or therapist because they naturally work comfortably with others.

Compliance and dominance folks want to get things done. Steadiness and influence people want to connect with others.

When you sort all of this out you have eight different roles that are different combinations of the four DISC styles.

Conductor - The high dominance oriented person is a conductor.

Persuader - Somebody who is a High-D and High-I is a persuader. You're going to find sales people a lot of times in the persuader category.

Promoter - Influence oriented people are called promoters.

Relater - A relater is someone who is diplomatic. Relaters get people thinking and talking together.

Supporter - A pure High-S person is going to be a supporter, best suited to supportive kinds of a roles.

Coordinator - A cross between steadiness and compliance is going to be a coordinator. A coordinator is going to understand what you feel and how you think, and they are also going to help you start to get things done.

Analyzer - A High-C, or high compliance oriented person might be described as an analyzer. An analyzer will look at the data, crunch the numbers, and understand what is going on by checking the available information. Not necessarily the people, but the information.

Implementer - At the top of wheel is a cross between the compliance and the dominance and that is your implementer. That is the person who gets the project started, keeps it on schedule and gets the project completed. That's what an implementer wants to do.

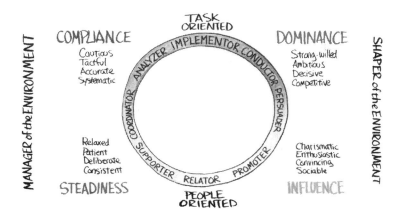

All of these different roles and different behavioral styles figure into a well-built organization. One person cannot be all things. That is the key takeaway here. If you are a promoter or maybe a persuader, you are not going to be comfortable and happy doing the job of accounting and bookkeeping. You are not going to be satisfied in an analyzer role. If your natural style is supporter, you will find it difficult to take on the conductor role because it is outside your behavioral style.

The more time you have to spend outside your DISC style, the more stress you will feel at work. Think of it as driving a car that pulls to the left a little bit. You always have to keep pressure on the steering wheel to keep the car going straight down the road and that fatigues you after a while.

What we want to do is employ people who are naturally going to fit the roles we need on our team. If I hire somebody for accounting, I want an analyzer. If I hire somebody for sales, I want a persuader. If I hire somebody for human resources I want a supporter, and so forth.

You can take your very own DISC Assessment for free at www.goalboss.com/disc. It takes about nine minutes and gives you an opportunity to see yourself in ways you might not have seen before.

Key Takeaways

In the space below, write your Key Takeaways from this chapter.

_____

_____

_____

_____

_____

_____

_____

_____

_____

_____

_____

_____

_____

_____

CHAPTER EIGHT

Great Leaders Know Themselves

We don't know what we don't know, as the saying goes. When it comes to self-knowledge, it's the things that you don't know that can hold you back the most. In an effort to reduce the number of things we don't know, let's look at different types of self-knowledge and break out what we know into different categories. Then we will cross-reference a thing or two. We will call the first category "known to self." Things that you know about yourself. The next category are things that are "known to others." If you cross-reference things that are known to self and things that are known to others, we end up with "public" information. For example: if I know I'm six feet one and you know I'm six feet one, then everybody knows that about me. It is public knowledge.

Taking this a step further, let us look at things that are known to self, but not known to others. Things that you know about yourself, and others do not. You are probably thinking of something like that now. Naturally, you know things about yourself that others do not and that is how it should be. We all have secrets. We call that category "private."

The next category are things about you that are unknown to you and unknown to others. You don't know some things about yourself, and other people don't know them either. These things are a "mystery". We don't know what we don't know.

The last category is the most important as we think about ways to grow as leaders, improve professionally, and be more useful to the people around us. These are the things that are known to other people, but not known to you! Things about you that everyone else knows, and you don't. Think about that! Everyone knows something about you… except you. Yikes!

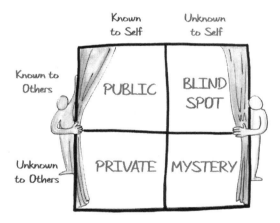

We call this category the "blind spot". Your blind spots are the very important because you have qualities and behaviors that everyone sees and deals with. Everyone but you. What we are focused on in particular are the blind spots that are holding you back. Characteristics about your behavior, how you communicate, how you react and respond, how you relate to your teammates that trip you up. Unhappily, you are completely unaware of these blind spots.

It takes a really good reason to go looking for blind spots. Our blind spots are often the things we want to know about the least. That is one of the reasons that we don't go after these things in the first place. It is human nature to ignore them.

Your blind spots are where most of your opportunities for growth can be found. Usually it is no fun, not comfortable to learn about a blind spot. There may be considerable discomfort that goes along with these discoveries. Not only for you, but also for the person with the courage to shine a light on things you don't know about you.

This model provides a powerful way of understanding our relationships with ourselves and others. It was created by psychologists Joseph Luft (1916–2014) and Harrington Ingham (1916–1995) in 1955. Luft and Ingham named this model the Johari Window after combining their first names, Joe and Harrington.

Underlying the purpose and goal of this book is exploring ways to help you illuminate your blind spots and move past the things you didn't know were slowing you down. We will look at different tools you can use to find out where your blind spots are, and how they are holding you back. We will present a simple method for deciding what to do about your blind spots. Goal Boss is about taking action. As leaders, we need to know what people see in us. We need to know what our behavior looks like to the rest of the world. Whenever we learn about one of those things, we have an opportunity to grow. Remember this: knowledge without action is useless. Developing your leadership skills is simple. It is not easy but it is straightforward. Growth as a leader is about action!

Key Takeaways

In the space below, write your Key Takeaways from this chapter.

_____

_____

_____

_____

_____

_____

_____

_____

_____

_____

_____

_____

_____

_____

CHAPTER NINE

Setting Goals

You are ten times more likely to achieve a goal if you write it down. The achievement of your goals, and therefore your success, increases even more when you share your goals with other people.  Especially those people who have a vested interest in your success. Your teammates need to know your goals so they can help hold you accountable.

The Goal Boss Leadership System has three parts. You have been introduced to Key Metrics. The second part of the Goal Boss Leadership System is setting and achieving goals. How do you do that really successfully?

If you write down a goal down and share it with somebody, does that change your responsibilities with regard to achieving it? If you know that you are ten times more likely to get something done by writing it down and sharing it with someone, and you don't write it down and don't share it with someone, what does that tell you about the level of commitment to the goal?

If you have a goal that you want to achieve, you must adopt a system for recording and sharing your goals with the people who matter. Share your goals with someone in your group because this greatly increases your chances of success. Let's look now at three tools you can use and three ways of looking at and setting goals that can make your goals more attainable.

SMART Goals

The first rule of goal setting is SMART. If you have been in business for any period of time you probably know what a SMART goal is but let's review just in case. SMART is an acronym that stands for Specific, Measurable, Attainable, Relevant, and Time Bound.

Specific

When you set a goal, it needs to be specific. Clearly express what the goal is. As an example, let us say that my goal is to finish the goal setting video and load into the Goal Boss Learning System. That is my goal. It is specific. What am I going to do? I am going to finish recording the goal setting video and load it into the Goal Boss Learning System. That is a clear definition of what I want to accomplish.

Measurable

The completion of a goal must be measurable. In this example, my goal is measurable because an objective observer with access to the data can log into the Goal Boss Learning System and see that the video is there. If they are really thorough they can watch the video and see if it is finished. Now I have a specific way to measure my goal: finish the goal setting video and load it into the Goal Boss Learning System. It is objectively measurable because anyone can know if it is done simply by looking.

Attainable

Is the goal attainable? Is it reasonable to expect that I can get there from here? In this case, I know the material. I have taught, coached, and lectured on this topic thousands of times. I have the technical capabilities and the equipment in my studio to make the goal setting video. I know how long it is going to take me to do it. I have the required time and I'm motivated. So, yes. I believe it is an attainable goal. I can get this done. I am going to have to work hard at it, but I can get it done.

Relevant

Is the goal relevant? Does it matter? Will achieving this goal to positively impact my Key Metrics? Is this goal relevant to the Key Metrics I have identified as being critical to the success of my organization? If I achieve this goal, is it going to move the needle on one of the important things in my business? Finishing the goal setting video and loading it up to the Goal Boss Learning System will allow me to share this information with thousands of people I couldn't reach before. Since my mission is to share the Goal Boss Leadership System at every opportunity, this goal is particularly relevant. This will move the needle on the things that matter most. When you think about relevant, think about Key Metrics.

Time Bound

Is the goal time bound? When am I going to get this done? The goal is specific. The only thing left to be certain about is when. Goals without deadlines are not goals. A task without a due date is due never. If you do not have a specific due date, you do not ever, ever have to do it. Every single goal you set should be time bound. Goals need a month, a day and a year that they are due. If your goal is not achieved by midnight on that month, day, year, then it is late. SMART goals get done. If your goals are not SMART, then maybe they are not goals at all.

Goal Certainty

Goal certainty it is what it sounds like. It is the level of certainty you have that you are going to achieve your goal. As another example, let's say that I have a goal of converting one cubic foot of oxygen into carbon dioxide in the next thirty days. It is specific. Given the proper equipment, you could measure how much oxygen I have converted into carbon dioxide. It is achievable because I am a human being and that is how we breathe. It is an attainable goal because when I breathe I intake oxygen and output carbon dioxide. Safe to say, I am converting oxygen into CO2 all day, every day. Perhaps this goal is relevant in that regard. This goal is time bound, because it has a due date of thirty days from now. But what about the quality of this goal?

Sandbag Goals

I am one hundred percent certain that I can achieve my goal of converting a cubic foot of oxygen into CO2. Technically, it's a SMART goal. I am one hundred percent certain that I can achieve this goal. But what good does it do me to set a goal that I'm one hundred percent certain of achieving? Do I need to bother setting a goal that I am absolutely certain I can attain? In this case, I cannot stop myself from converting oxygen into CO2, it's what humans do.

A goal that you are one hundred percent certain of achieving has a one hundred percent level of goal certainty. You might call that a sandbag goal. Setting a sandbag goal is not going to make a difference because it is going to get done no matter what. Sandbag goals live at the one hundred percent end of the goal certainty graph.

Unrealistic Goals

What about a goal with zero percent certainty? Let us go back to my first goal example, which was to complete the goal setting video and get it loaded up to the Goal Boss Learning System. But let's change the timing and say that I want to complete the goal in the next fifteen seconds. No chance! I am not going to be able to get that done in the next fifteen seconds because I have already used up that fifteen seconds writing about the goal. I have already run out of time.

What possible reason would someone have for setting a goal they know they cannot achieve? Surprisingly, those reasons exist. Mostly, people set unrealistic, pie-in-the-sky goals to impress or distract others. I have seen people in business meetings promise anything just to get out of an uncomfortable conversation, or to momentarily impress others.

"I'm going to exceed my sales quota by two hundred percent this month," Bill declared.

"Okay, Bill," I'd reply. "Given the fact that you haven't gotten higher than forty percent of your quota in the last twelve months, do you think it's realistic to promise four times that in the next thirty days? What's changed?"

Goals like Bill's unrealistic goal are usually ignored because everyone in the room knows they are unrealistic. People figure, "Oh, that's just Bill." Or, even worse, someone might take Bill at his word. What if the operations department decides to ramp up production to meet Bill's new sales? Yikes!

So, an unrealistic goal at zero certainty doesn't do you any good and a sandbag goal at 100% goal certainty doesn't either. Where is the sweet spot? Where do you want to be in terms of goal certainty and why?

The answer is eighty percent. When you set a goal try to do it so that you are about eighty percent certain you will achieve it. You have already done the first test which is to make sure that it's a SMART goal. Next you want to be about eighty percent certain that you can achieve the goal. And here is why: if you are eighty percent certain that you can achieve a goal, you can bring confidence to it. You are not setting yourself up to fail. On the other hand, with eighty percent goal certainty, there is still a small chance that you might not get there. You are going to have to focus and work hard. You are going to have to bring your passion, your commitment, and your energy, to achieving this goal. You are going to have to stretch outside your comfort zone to achieve this goal because it is an eighty percent certain goal. That will make you grow. That will force you to work harder, which will make you better at what you do and grow as the person you are.

When you set an eighty percent certain goal your teammates know that four out of five times you are going to come through for them. If you set an eighty percent certain goal and your teammates are relying on you, they know there is a good chance that you will deliver. They also know you are pushing yourself as hard as you can. You are not sandbagging, not laying back. If your team knows you are going to succeed four out of five times, that represents a high level of dependability. You are bringing your very best. Those behaviors will foster teamwork and help your organization become more successful. That is what goal certainty is. Run the goal certainty test on every goal you set. When you are working with your teammates, run the goal certainty test on their goals to ask them what level of certainty they have. Challenge your teammates. It helps them get better just as when they challenge you it helps you get better.

Now you have SMART goals and Goal Certainty. These are proven tools that you can bring to goal achievement. The final test to be sure your goal is excellent involves a bold thought experiment.

Eulogy Goals

Imagine that you just found out that in thirty days you are going to die. That's right. Pretend you have thirty days to live and there's nothing that anybody can do about it and you just found this out right now. That is the first condition of our thought experiment. We do this exercise a lot at Goal Boss workshops and events. I know the next condition of this exercise has to be: you still have to go to work! The third condition is: in thirty-two days, we are going to have your funeral. Your family, your friends, your teammates and your co-workers will be there. The only thing we will talk about at your funeral when we are celebrating your many contributions and your amazing life will be the goals that you set and achieved in the last thirty days you were here. Nothing else.

Given this situation and these parameters, what kind of goals are you going to set? What kind of things do you want people to remember about you if you have only thirty days to make it happen?

I have talked to thousands of people about this particular issue, and asked them what kind of goals are you going to set if you have thirty days? The answer that I get more often than any other answer is: I'm going to set amazing goals. If I have thirty days left and if I am going to be remembered for what happens in the next thirty days, you can bet I am going to  work incredibly hard. I am going to change the world. I am going to move the needle on the things I have identified as the most important things for myself, my family, my teammates.

That is what we tend to do when we know we are running out of time. It changes our perspective, it clarifies what is important. As soon as I know I am going to run out of time, I get to work. I get busy because I want to make a difference. I want to be remembered. I want to leave this place better than I found it. That is always the answer I get.

Here is my next question: how do you know you don't only have thirty days? Do you know how much time you have? How long will you wait to start doing things you want to be remembered for? Everyone runs out of time. No one knows when. When you set goals, make sure you are setting them in a way that would make the people around you the proudest. At Goal Boss, we call these Eulogy Goals. Run the eulogy goal test on every goal you set to help you be sure you are bringing it all day, every day.

Those are the three tools that make up the Goal Boss goal-setting system. Make sure that your goals are SMART. Specific, measurable, attainable, relevant, time-bound. Make sure that you bring eighty percent goal certainty to every single goal you set. Make sure that you are pushing as hard as you should and make sure there is a four out of five chance that you are going to achieve your goals. Finally, do the Eulogy Goal test. Make your contributions to your team matter. Make your achievements impactful. Push yourself hard because at the end of the day, either you gave it your all or you didn't and it is so much nicer to feel you did.

Key Takeaways

In the space below, write your Key Takeaways from this chapter.

_____

_____

_____

_____

_____

_____

_____

_____

_____

_____

_____

_____

_____

_____

_____

CHAPTER TEN

Team Problem Solving

K ey Metrics, Goals, and Team Problem Solving are the three parts of the Goal Boss Leadership System. Now we will take a closer look at Team Problem Solving and become experts in this methodology. Team Problem Solving is a method for solving problems while achieving goals designed to move the needle on the things that matter most, those Key Metrics.

Perhaps you remember the movie Apollo 13. A wonderful story based on one of the most stirring adventures ever in human achievement. About 56 hours after lift-off, Apollo 13 experienced a series of life threatening problems. Houston-we-have-a-problem level problems! There was a scene in the film where Gene Kranz, the flight director, gathered a room full of rocket scientists. Then on the overhead projector he

drew a picture of the earth, a picture of the Moon and a line that showed how far the spaceship was going to get with the existing power and resources it had. Then Gene said to the team: "Okay gentlemen. How do we get them the rest of the way home?"

The rocket scientists then used the team problem solving methodology. A brilliant way to batch process conversations, questions, answers and suggested action steps to get to the heart of an issue. Fast.

The Goal Boss Team Problem Solving method takes ten minutes and starts off with one person stating a problem in the form of a "How to" question. The how to question simply asks how to solve a problem, whatever the problem may be.

The person with the problem is the Team Problem Solving Client. Everyone else involved is a teammate. Once you have determined your how to question, the Team Problem Solving event takes only ten minutes. Let's break down the timing.

Background and Facts – One Minute

For the first minute the client will state the Background and Facts of the problem. Sixty seconds is all the client has to tell the story of what is wrong and how it is affecting the team. When that minute is up, that minute is up. Team Problem Solving is a carefully timed event.

Questions and Answers – Two Minutes

The next two minutes is dedicated to Questions and Answers. Because time is short, questions must be succinct and to the point. The client answers each question as quickly and efficiently as he can. Then someone else will ask a question, and so on. For two minutes, questions and answers continue so the team has more information to use solving the problem. When two minutes is up, it is time to move on to the next step.

Suggested Action Steps – Five Minutes

In this phase, the team goes around the room giving everyone involved an opportunity to suggest action steps to the client. Each and every teammate simply tells the client what to do to solve the problem. During this five minutes the client does not speak! The client simply listens and writes down the suggested action steps everyone else in the room proposes. The client may not agree with every idea offered. There is no judgement, the client is just writing everything down, gathering up as many suggestions as possible.

Stop and Jot – 2 Minutes

The last two minutes are called stop and jot. The client takes the list of suggested action steps and decides which actions they will take. Committing to an action step is simple. The client simply writes a date next to each action step they will pursue. Either the date they will start, or a date that item will be done. We call this phase 'stop and jot' because it only takes a couple of minutes to do it. The client rarely chooses everything on the list and might even add one or two things because ideas have occurred during the process. At the end of the two minutes, the client will have chosen the action steps. Then the client tells the team which suggestions they are going to pursue. Those action steps are set as goals for the client.

Total Time – 10 Minutes

Team Problem Solving takes ten minutes. We batch process all four steps. To recap, if I am the client I will give my team all the information I can in one minute. Next, in two minutes, my team will ask me as many questions as they can. Then, for five minutes the team is going to make suggestions to me. They will just tell me what to do. Finally, in the last two minutes, I will decide which of those suggestions I will take on as action steps. I make a commitment to myself and my team that I am going to get those things done.

The Goal Boss Platform has several tools to help you do this. The first and most simple one, obviously, is the team problem solving worksheet at www.goalboss.com. Just print it out and do it. The Goal Boss Platform provides an online team meeting facilitator with the Team Problem Solving function built right in. You can do as many team problem-solving sessions as you need during a Goal Boss Meeting. The output can be saved to the Goal Boss Platform. The action steps you choose can be saved as goals. Team Problem Solving sessions should be recorded in your Goal Boss Meeting minutes so everyone on the team knows what happened. This is a proven process to solve problems, drive accountability and get results.

Key Takeaways

In the space below, write your Key Takeaways from this chapter.

TEAM PROBLEM SOLVING

MOON

Apollo 13

EARTH

1) Background & Facts (1 min)

2) Clarifying Questions (2 min)

3) Suggested Action Steps (5 min)

4) Stop and Jot (2 min)

team problem solving worksheet

name   **date**

write your how to question

1. problem background & facts (1 min)
2. questions from the team (2 min)
3. write suggested action steps (5 min)   4. stop & jot (2 min)

goal boss

CHAPTER ELEVEN

Five Keys to Leadership

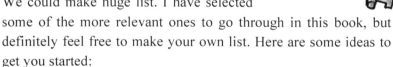

When you go to work, what are the kinds of things you do there? Let's make a list of the tasks we do and the interactions we have at work. I have asked this question in a lot of workshops, and I get a variety of answers. We could make huge list. I have selected some of the more relevant ones to go through in this book, but definitely feel free to make your own list. Here are some ideas to get you started:

Meetings. We all have meetings when we go to work, that is just part of the business environment. Emails. We all write emails. Hiring. We hire people a lot of the time. The flipside of hiring is firing. Planning. Some of us do business planning. Strategy. Writing. We write proposals for internal use or for customers. We train our people to do great work. We handle legal issues when they arise. Maybe we sit down and just catch up on the industry. Building consensus, making sure that people are working together. Introducing people to one another. Keeping the wheels on the wagon. Handling benefits and payroll is certainly part of running an organization. Customer service. Customers are great and sometimes they need help. Delegating. Getting things done without doing things yourself. I am a devoted fan of delegation. Negotiating, forecasting and career counseling. This is just a partial list of things we do at work. If we were in a room together we could go through and create a list of many more things we all do on a daily basis.

It can definitely get overwhelming. When we make this list in a Goal Boss workshop, people start to feel just that. Overwhelmed. When that happens, I slow everybody down and say "Don't freak out. It is okay because here is the good news: you only do five things when you go to work." Only five things, ever. Here are the five things: communicating, planning, organizing, controlling and leading.

THE 5 KEYS TO LEADERSHIP

Meetings	communicating	Reading
Email		Building Consensus
Hiring	planning	Introducing People
Firing		Benefits & Payroll
Planning	organizing	Customer Service
Strategy		Delegating
Writing Proposals	controlling	Negotiating
Training Employees		Forecasting
Handling Legal Issues	leading	Career Counseling

As you develop your expertise in these five areas you will get better, stronger and more effective as a leader. Everything on our long list will fall into one of these five categories. Everything.

Those meetings and that email, those are communicating. When we hire somebody, that is a function of organizing. The definition of organizing is to align resources for maximum achievement. When you fire somebody, that is controlling. The definition of controlling is to compare performance to objectives and take appropriate action. Sometimes firing is the appropriate action. Planning is planning. Strategy is also planning. When we are writing proposals for people that is a subset of communicating. When we are training employees, we are organizing. We are aligning resources for maximum achievement. We are providing our people the skills they need to perform productively.

Handling legal issues is another controlling function. Reading may fall into more than one category. When I am reading I am thinking about how I can use what I am learning in the future. That is planning. Building consensus is straight up leadership. Leading is all about is getting people on the same page. Introducing people to one another is also leading. Benefits and payroll is organizing. Customer service is controlling. If a customer has a problem we fix it. Delegating is also organizing. Getting things done without doing things yourself. I say that over and over again. Negotiating is probably leadership. Forecasting is planning. Career counseling is organizing.

THE 5 KEYS TO LEADERSHIP

Meetings	communicating	Reading
Email		Building Consensus
Hiring	planning	Introducing People
Firing		Benefits & Payroll
Planning	organizing	Customer Service
Strategy		Delegating
Writing Proposals	controlling	Negotiating
Training Employees		Forecasting
Handling Legal Issues	leading	Career Counseling

When you look at our list from this perspective, you will find everything you do falls into one of these five categories.

Exercise

On a sheet of paper, make your own list of every single task you do at work.

Put each activity into one of these five categories.

Give yourself a one-to-ten score on how well you do each task.

This can help you identify your strengths and your opportunities for improvement in each of these five areas.

Commit to learning as much as you can about strengths and weaknesses as a leader. Do you suppose other people would see your strengths and opportunities the same way you do? Think back to the Johari window, which we discussed not too long ago. You will recall that people see you differently than you see yourself. The key to becoming an effective leader is self-awareness. Leadership requires the courage to step up and do whatever it takes to shine a light on your blind spots. Successful leaders push through the discomfort that comes with personal and professional growth. As irony would have it, the key to self-knowledge usually lies in asking someone else.

That is why 360 feedback is so valuable. Goal Boss Certified Coaches will go through and read every bit of the feedback we get from other people and we categorize it into one of the five areas so we know where the opportunity for improvement lies.

The encouraging news about the Five Keys to Leadership is that communicating, planning, organizing, controlling, and leading are all skills. They are not talents or gifts. If you have discovered that you have opportunities to grow in the area of communicating, you can develop and improve your communication skills. Same thing goes for planning, organizing, controlling and leading. I have yet to meet someone who cannot dramatically improve their leadership skills through this process. This book and the Goal Boss Leadership System are about developing leadership skills by taking action.

Key Takeaways

In the space below, write your Key Takeaways from this chapter.

_____

_____

_____

_____

_____

_____

_____

_____

_____

_____

_____

_____

_____

_____

CHAPTER TWELVE

Communicating Skills

L et's review the five keys to leadership. Communicating, planning, organizing, controlling and leading. We have discussed how everything you do as a leader falls into one of these five categories. We have talked about how different words and phrases in our emails and conversations can be markers for opportunities for improvement in each of these five areas.

To improve as a leader, you must continually increase your skills in the five keys to leadership.

Communicating is the first key to leadership because without expert communication skills, the other keys to leadership are rendered ineffective. The simplest definition of communicating I have found is to get someone to understand your thoughts, ideas, or feelings. When you can do that you open the door to new possibilities and potential. If, on the other hand, you struggle to make yourself understood, or if you let things like frustration or emotion cloud your message, then your leadership will suffer, and your career may falter. Communication is one of the Big Three Career Killers. When you reach the limit of your communication skills, that is where your career stalls. In order to grow personally and professionally, you will always be improving your communication skills.

The best news about communicating is that communicating is a skill. Unlike talents, which we are born with, skills can be taught, learned, and developed. You do not need to be a gifted, talented, natural communicator in order to be expert at communicating. Everyone can improve their communication skills. Becoming an expert communicator is well within your grasp. Let's get started.

The Communication Loop

Believe it or not, the way computers communicate sets an excellent standard we as communicating experts should all aspire to. Let's walk through an example.

If I want to send a message from my computer to your computer. I type up and format the message, then click send and cluster of data goes across the wire. When your computer gets the message it immediately sends back an ACK – or an acknowledgement - to let my computer know that it received the message. The computer that receives the data is capable of detecting if the message received was actually what the sending computer meant to send.

If the message is perfect, the computer that receives it knows that it's perfect, and ACKnowledges this event to the sending computer. No fuss, no muss, no emotion. Just ones and zeros, pretty much. Yay, computers!

If there is a problem with the message being received, the computer sends back a nACK - a "not acknowledged" message. Essentially, the computer is saying that it got something but the data is garbled and it's not exactly sure what it was sent. In this case, the sending computer will resend the message until it gets the ACK that it's looking for. The point of understanding this method of communication is that the communication between computers across a network is incredibly well-structured and reliable.

How does that compare to communication with people? Let's say for example that I want you to build me something. Let's pretend this communication is a cartoon. In my head is the widget that I would like you to build for me.

In a perfect world, like our computer messages, I'm going to send you that message and you're going to say "Oh, yeah, absolutely. I got that message. I can totally build you one of these. I understand exactly what you mean. I know what the shape and the color and the size of the widget is. I understand everything and I'm going to acknowledge that transmission."

Now, think about the real world. Think of the people you work with. Think of things that have been asked of you and things that you've asked of other people. How often do you get exactly what you asked for? Or do you ask for a specific thing and you get back something similar to what you were hoping for? It's kind of like what you asked for, but not exactly. And the ACK part rarely happens, if it all. So, you sent a message - in that message you asked for something and then the

receiver brought back something. And it's close, but not quite what you need. You never had a truly clear communication about what you wanted. Everyone involved meant well, but things went sideways just the same. Why? Because you never got the ACK, or the acknowledgement.

As the sender of the message, the person doing the communicating, you are responsible for the communication. You always own the success or failure of any communication you initiate. Just like the sending computer owns the success or failure of that communication. The difference is the receiving computer sends back constant feedback. It got the message, or it didn't get the message. It got this but it was incomplete. Please resend the message. What's more, computers just keep trying until they get it right. People don't usually do it that way… until they use the Communication Loop!

The Communication Loop

The Communication Loop solves the problem of garbled or incomplete communication. The Communication Loop makes it possible for you to be far more efficient in your communication. Since you know you are not going to get an automatic ACK back from most human beings, the only solution is to ask!

Request a playback. When you send a message to a coworker, "I want one of these, please." Always request a playback from them. There is very specific language that you can use for requesting playback when you send a message to someone. It is this:

"Could you play that back to me so I know I did a good job of communicating it?"

Let's unpack that language, because this is one of the most carefully constructed sentences in the Goal Boss Leadership System.

First of all, it is a question. More specifically, it is a request for help. You are asking for help from the person to whom you sent your message. "Could you play that back to me so I know I did a good job of communicating it?"

When you ask another person for help, chances are good that they will want to help you. A lot of times people assume they might be putting someone out. They might be inconveniencing them. But most people genuinely want to contribute. We all want to find ways to be helpful. We all want people to thank us for our help.

So, when you ask, "Can you play that back to me…," what you're saying is: "Could you please help me? Can you help me to make sure I did a good job?" You own the communication. You are responsible for making sure you did it well. If the other person does not get it, if they build you the wrong widget, that's on you.

The second half of the sentence is perhaps more important than the first. It reads, "…so I know I did a good job of communicating."

Again, you are making it crystal clear to the person you are communicating with that if this communication isn't effective, it is your responsibility. That is why you are asking for playback. This approach differs significantly from simply asking, "Got it?" Because that question lacks any detail. Asking someone if they "got it," is nearly meaningless. All they need to say is, "Yep," or

"Got it," and you have no idea what, if anything, the other person "got!" You are then living in hope. In business, hope is undiscovered disappointment.

Take the time to be absolutely sure that others know what you need and what you mean. It is a simple concept. When you start to use the Communication Loop, when you start to ask people to play it back, your effectiveness as a leader will measurably increase.

At first using the Communication Loop will be awkward. It will not feel natural, because it isn't. Others may be confused and they may ask whether you think they are an idiot. When that happens - and it might - you must address that straight up. Say "No, no, no. I don't think you are an idiot. If I thought that I would not have asked you anything in the first place. What I want to be sure of is did I do a good job communicating it because I want to set you up to succeed. That's the reason I am asking for the playback. Now, could you play that back to me so I know I did a good job of communicating?"

Asking someone for playback is a sign of respect. It is respect for the communication, it is respect for the thing that you want to get done and most importantly it is respect for the other person who is involved in this conversation.

Take the time to do this well. Take the time to get playback and your efficiency will increase. The respect you and your teammates share will increase. Morale will increase. Productivity will increase, and it all goes to the bottom line of your business. The Communication Loop is how high-performing teams and high-performing organizations accomplish things. Adopt this technique, and if you take nothing more from this book but the Communication Loop, it will pay off over and over again.

Communication Breakdown

Let's break down what the different pieces of a communication look like and see how they impact overall meaning. The three components of communication are content, which is the written word, the actual literal words. Next is verbal, that is the tone of voice in which the content is spoken. Third is the visual. Body language or other non-verbal cues.

These three components - content, verbal, and visual - make up one hundred percent of a given communication. If we unpack communication further, we learn how these three components are weighted. What impact does one component have in comparison to the others?

Content

Look at the content portion of a communication. How important is the written word alone? If you had only the words on this page to go by, how effective will the message be? In other words, will you truly understand what I mean simply by reading this sentence? What is left open to interpretation without any verbal or visual cues to go by? Just for fun, write down what percentage of the communication you believe is purely about the content? Keep in mind that content + verbal + visual = one hundred percent. Out of one hundred percent, how much true meaning is conveyed by just the content?

You may be surprised to learn that for most teams, the total value of the actual content - what is written down of a communication - ends up being seven percent of the total communication. If you give someone a memo that is just written, they are basically going to get about seven percent of your total meaning.

Verbal

Let's say I give you a compliment. Pretend that I say "Hey, you look great today," and my tone of voice is cheerful and upbeat. You have the content of the message, which are the literal words, as well as verbal cues to go by. I said a nice thing in nice tone of voice. However, you don't have any visual cues. From only tone and cadence of my voice when I say, "Hey you look great today", what do you suppose that means? It probably means that I think you look great today. The verbal tone of the communication, just my tone of voice and cadence, really change things. You may be surprised to know that the verbal component of a communication actually accounts for 38% of the total meaning of a spoken communication.

Visual

Now, let's add a visual component to that same message. When I say, "Hey you look great today," you can see that my shoulders are shrugged and I am looking off to the side and rolling my eyes. Adding the visual component to our otherwise friendly message changes everything, doesn't it?

Here's the real kicker - a full 55% of a communication's meaning is in visual cues and body language. If you have a choice between sending an email and walking down the hall and talking to somebody what should you choose?

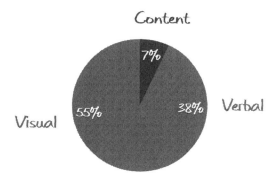

If you want to get the full value of a communication and be able to really leverage the communication loop that we talked about before, you might want to get out of your chair to walk down the hall and speak face to face. Talk directly to the person because 93% of what you communicate is in how you say it and what you look like when you say it.

Comfortable Words

William Shakespeare wrote "Speak comfortable words." The intent of communication is to get someone to understand your thoughts, ideas, or feelings. Clarity figures into this greatly. Going back to Shakespeare's advice to speak comfortable words, it is helpful to note the difference between plain and fancy.

In business, you might have survived a fancy conversation or two in meetings where the goal is to impress or even baffle other people. Generally speaking, these conversations are not productive. Sometimes they can even be disruptive or destructive to the organization. If you find yourself at risk of being buried in fancy words, draw a line down the middle of a sheet of paper, creating two columns. Write the word "Plain" at the top of one column and "Fancy" at the top of the other. Make tic marks to compare how many fancy words and how many plain words you hear. The fancier the words you hear, the less likely any real communication is happening.

Sometimes people go to great lengths to impress. To baffle with BS rather than to encourage you to understand their thoughts, ideas, or feelings. If you are smart and confused at the same time, there is something wrong about the communication going on. It is not important to amaze people in business meetings. It is important to communicate with them. Communication wants comfortable words.

Avoid fancy talk. Do not be impressed or distracted by the elaborate presentations. Be the person in the room who asks simple questions. Be the person in the room who uses one and two syllable words rather than multisyllabic sophisticated discourse. Do not attempt to baffle people to impress or suppress them. It is unconvincing and a waste of time. Be a leader. Get the point across and let them decide whether or not your message is impressive. As Shakespeare said, speak comfortable words.

Key Takeaways

In the space below, write your Key Takeaways from this chapter.

_____

_____

_____

_____

_____

_____

_____

_____

_____

_____

_____

_____

_____

CHAPTER THIRTEEN

Keys to Communicating

Communicating expertly requires that you excel in four main areas: planning, sending, receiving, and reviewing. As you learn and continue to master communicating using this method, you and the people you work with will get more accomplished with better results and fewer mistakes and misunderstandings.

Planning

Before you do anything, make a plan for it. The best way to create a plan is to ask the very first question from the very beginning of this book - the first question we ask in anything is...

What's the Goal?

What is your goal for delivering this communication? What do you want to happen because you communicated this thought, this idea or these feelings? What's the goal? That is always the best first question.

Know Your Audience

Think about who you are going to deliver this message to. If you are going to deliver a message to your fifteen-year-old son, it probably should be a different presentation - a different language and tone - than if you are going to deliver a message to the CEO of a billion-dollar corporation. Every conversation is going to be different based on the audience. Knowing your audience is part of your planning. What motivates your audience? What do they expect to receive from this communication? Build your conversation to serve the other person. Do you know their DISC style? That would help a lot! Do not make it about you. Make it about your audience.

How Will the Message Best Be Received?

This is practical, tactical question. Is the person that you want to communicate with really busy? Would it be better if you sent them an email? Would it be better to call them on the phone? Do they prefer a text? What is the effective medium for you to use for this message? How you send the message will tend to determine how the conversation goes. If someone wants a text from you, you are going keep it tight. Very tight. When communicating with a "High S" DISC style, they may prefer to sit down and have a conversation. Always consider the behavioral style of the person you are talking to. These choices are important and making the right ones will save you time. Do they want you to just get to the point or do they want you to build on one point after another so that they can reach their own conclusion? Give those factors some thought before you start message delivery.

Timing is Everything

When is the best time to reach this person? Try to be considerate of their schedule, both in terms of the best time to reach them and the amount of time your message will take to read, hear, see, or otherwise process. If you are communicating in person or by phone, consider starting the conversation by asking, "Have I reached you at a bad time?" Timing is everything. Make it your business to know when the person you are communicating with is best able to receive your communication. What works best for them?

What are the Key Takeaways?

Planning communication is about finding ways to make things turn out the way you want. Make sure you know exactly what the receiver of your communication should conclude at the end. What are the key takeaways that you want the receiver to get from your perspective?

This process may seem tedious at first. Stick with it, and remember: Prior proper planning prevents poor performance!

Sending

With your careful communication plan laid out, it is time to send the message. But first, ask permission. "Have you got a second? Do you mind? Can we schedule a call?" Find a time and ask for permission. Schedule your message. If you are sending an email message and it is going to be long and detailed, perhaps send a shorter email first and ask for permission to send the longer one. It will be easier for the receiver to read your message if they know it is coming. They are not going to be surprised by it. So, ask for permission. Always a good idea.

Share the Goal

More often than not, I will start an email with: 'Dear so-and-so, the goal for this email is...' If you read a news article, the end is the first part you read. The headline states the whole point of the article and then the details follow. Don't bury the lead! Share the goal up front.

Choose Words Carefully

Build a whole sentence in your head and run it through. Don't blurt stuff out. When you get excited, you might talk fast. You might say things you will regret. Particularly when you're answering questions, if this is a back-and-forth conversation, take five seconds after someone asks you a question to think about how you are going to answer. This master strategy of communicating will help you achieve two things.

First, you will not step on your own toes nearly as often because you will give yourself a chance to think before you speak.

Second by taking just a few seconds and letting a bit of silence into the conversation, you are demonstrating that you are a thoughtful person. You are a person who thinks before they speak. This simple strategy will set you apart from those who cannot wait for their turn to talk.

Bring Action Steps and Solutions

An expert communicator will always show up for the conversation prepared to suggest action steps to achieve the goal. If you are asked, make suggestions. If you are not asked to make suggestions for action steps, ask for permission to do so. Go back to the first thing on the list. "May I make a suggestion about how we might accomplish this?" After you ask, wait for them to answer. If, and only if, they say yes, make your suggestions. Communicating is about respect. Communicating is about empathy. It is about knowing what the other person needs and trying to find ways to give that to them. Communication is not about getting your own way. If you start with that attitude, you will put the receiver on the defensive. It is difficult to get something that you want when the person you want it from is defensive. So, go in with an open mind and that will help everyone in the conversation to stay open.

Ask for Feedback

After you deliver the message, be sure to ask for feedback. Say, "I'm working on my communication skills. Can you give me a little feedback? How did I do with my communication? What worked for you? What didn't work for you? How can I do better in communicating with you in the future?"

If you ask people for help, they will want to help you. If you ask people for help, especially in areas where it will ease their burden, they will want to help you even more.

Use the Communication Loop

Don't forget the magic words of two-way communication. *Can you play that back to me so I know I did a good job of communicating it?* Make sure you do not live in hope that someone understood you. You put a lot of thought into delivering your message. You deserve to know if you did a good job. The recipient of your communication deserves to understand your message the way you intended. That is what the communication loop does. When you do the things an expert communicator does, you become an expert at communicating.

Receiving

Suppose somebody comes to you with a communication. They have gone through all of the steps to send you a message. They planned their communication with you. They asked for permission. They shared the goal. Now, they are here and ready to choose their words carefully.

When you are the receiver of a communication, how can your participation and performance influence the outcome? How can you help the sender to do a good job?

Listen Actively.

Active listening is profoundly uncomplicated. It starts with looking the person in the eye when they talk. That allows you to get the whole communication: content, verbal and visual. If you are on the phone, close your eyes and listen. This blocks out any conflicting visual cues and helps you better understand what is being said. Repeating what they say in little increments will make sure you are getting the message as it is intended.

Know the Goal

At the beginning of any conversation, the first question should always be, "What's the goal?" Make sure you know what it is. If the sender has not made it clear, just ask. "I am glad we are having this talk. Let me ask you this: what is the goal for our conversation today?" If you are in a business conversation and you do not know the goal, stop! Ask what is the goal?

Keep an Open Mind

In business when we have our thing to do and someone else has their thing to do, we can get defensive. We begin trying to protect our position and it slows us down and prevents us from hearing people. Keep an open mind. Do not judge. Wait until the other person stops talking before you begin to formulate your response. It costs you nothing to imagine a world the way the other person wants it to be. Considering an opposing point of view is an important leadership skill.

Participate Without Taking Over

When you are the receiver of a message, make it a general rule to let the other person have four sentences for every one sentence you have. Remember the Pareto Principle? Use the twenty percent of your participation in this conversation wisely. Twenty percent talking, eighty percent listening. Twenty percent making suggestions, eighty percent asking questions. Don't take over the conversation. Develop the skills of listening, asking questions, and bringing out the best in the people around you.

Focus on the Sender

Put your phone away. Do not text, check email or do anything else that signals distraction. Do not allow distractions when you are listening to someone else. Texting or checking email when someone is talking to you is not merely impolite. It erodes trust. Being just a little bit distracted signals to someone that they are not important in your world, or even in this conversation. You do not want people to feel that. You want people to know you are interested in what they have to say. You are listening. You are not judging. Focus on the person in the conversation. Your goal in every conversation is to bring out the best in the other person. That is the way you are at your best. Being in a conversation is an active, energetic thing. It is not automatic. Listening is not easy to do well, which is why so many of us do not do it well. It is so much more than just not making sound, and even that is sometimes hard to accomplish.

Acknowledge and empathize with the sender. Put yourself in their shoes. Imagine what it feels like to be them. Imagine what it is like to have their job, to have their task, to have their problems, to have their goals. Put yourself in their shoes.

There is a technique that you can use to almost instantly know how someone is feeling. You want to be careful with this so as not to offend. If you can see the expression on someone's face and you can find a way, at least mentally, to mimic that facial expression you will know how they feel. The muscles in your face reflect emotion. Big emotions and little micro expressions as well. If you look at someone's face and try to mimic the face that they are making, you are going to start to feel the emotions associated with the expression. Try it sometime when you are out people watching. When you are in the mall or the train station or someplace like that. Try to mimic the expressions of total strangers and you will start to know how they feel. You can develop the skill of empathy.

Use the Communication Loop.

I know I say this a lot. Take ownership of receiving the message. You do not have to wait for the other person to ask. You can ask, "Can I play that back for you just so I know I heard you accurately?" Actively engage with people when you communicate. It may take a little bit longer in the moment but it saves a lot of time in the long run. It will quickly develop a reputation for you as a leader. Someone who really gets it. The most interesting people do not talk much. They listen. Interesting people draw you out, they ask you questions. Do the work. Be determined to become an amazing communicator.

Reviewing

When it's all said and done, whether you are the sender or the receiver, before you wrap up a conversation, just take a minute and do a quick review.

Was the Communication Effective?

Again, just ask. "Was this communication effective? Do you feel like we achieved our goal? Did we get what we want out of this?" Remember, you started with a goal for the conversation. Did you get to the goal?

Ask for Feedback

Simply say, "I really appreciate your listening. Thank you for your time. Can you suggest ways that I might do a better job of communicating next time?" This is your golden opportunity to build trust, learn about yourself, and increase your invaluable communicating skills. So, ask!

Coach Your Teammates

Help your teammates to develop their communication skills. Be a coach. Ask questions, suggest ideas, make a copy of the keys to communicating and hand it to someone. Help your teammates improve their communication skills and they will help you.

Set Goals to Improve Your Skills

When somebody does give you candid timely feedback, take it to heart. Take action. Perhaps a teammate suggested that your presentation could have been better or it might have been more helpful if you brought other information. Write those things down and set a professional growth goal. Set goals and take action to improve your communication skills. Opportunities for improvement are just that. Opportunities!

Communication is one of The Big Three Career Killers. When you reach the limit of your ability to communicate, that is where your career stops. Wherever you are, that is where you stop. You must continue improving your communication skills every single day if you want to keep growing professionally and personally. If you study the people who are the most successful, the people you admire the most, I think you will find those people are expert at communicating and they keep getting better. That is my goal for you, and that is what I want you to learn from the lessons on communicating.

Key Takeaways

In the space below, write your Key Takeaways from this chapter.

_____

_____

_____

_____

_____

_____

_____

_____

_____

_____

_____

_____

_____

_____

KEYS TO COMMUNICATING

Planning
- What's the goal?
- Who is your audience?
- How will your message best be received?
- What about timing?
- What are the key takeaways?

Sending
- Ask for permission.
- Share the goal.
- Choose words carefully.
- Suggest possible action steps to achieve the goal.
- Ask for feedback.
- Use the Communication Loop.

Receiving
- Listen. Actively!
- Ask – What's the goal?
- Keep an open mind. Don't judge.
- Participate in the conversation without taking over.
- Focus on the sender, especially in person.
- Acknowledge and empathize with the sender.
- Use the Communication Loop (ACK!).

Reviewing
- Was the communication effective?
- Ask for candid, timely feedback.
- Coach your teammates in communicating skills.
- Set goals to improve how well you communicate.

goal boss

CHAPTER FOURTEEN

Prior Proper Planning

P rior proper planning prevents poor performance. Show me a failing business, or a team that has lost their way, and I will show you an organization without a plan. What better way to deploy your newfound expertise in the art and science of communicating - at getting other people to understand your thoughts, ideas, or feelings - than by having a rock-solid plan to share with and inspire your team. Welcome to the second key to leadership: planning.

Dwight Eisenhower said, "In preparing for battle I have always found that plans are useless, but planning is indispensable."

What do you suppose Dwight meant when he said that? Planning is indispensable, but plans are useless. If plans are useless in battle, why plan in the first place? The answer involves focus, problem solving, creativity, and how your brain manages those things. When you have a goal and a plan to get from here to your goal, you automatically engage the problem solving and visualization parts of your brain. In particular, you engage your reticular activating system, or RAS. Your reticular activating system is the part of your brain that filters the information coming into your brain all day, every day. Without it, you would hear, see, feel, and taste everything all at once. The RAS helps you ignore things that are not relevant, and it helps you focus on things that are. You would not notice a cat sitting in a tree if the house next to that tree was on fire. The burning house would also become less important as soon as you heard the horn of the fire truck which was about to run you down because you were standing in the street. Depending on your focus, depending on the thing you have told your brain is most important, your Reticular Activating System will automatically help you move toward that thing. That is why you need a plan.

Beyond the obvious step-by-step instructions of getting from here to there, a plan helps you start to see your goal come true before it actually happens. You can picture it in your head. Even if the plan doesn't work out exactly the way you want, your brain will automatically adjust to keep you moving towards your goal. That is why setting a goal up front makes it far more likely that you will achieve the goal. Setting the goal puts your reticular activating system in motion. It gets your brain, even your subconscious brain, working for you.

Creating a plan to achieve your goal gives you more flexibility and opportunities for innovation when you run into problems. You will always run into problems when you are trying to accomplish something. Sometimes the problems are small, and sometimes they are big. Either way, when you have a goal and a plan, you can problem solve your way to that goal just about every time. The definition of the word 'planning' is "Defining a set of actions as a strategy to achieve specific goals." That is what we are going to talk about in this chapter. Your goal is the What. Your plan is the How.

Your One Page Plan

How do you decide what are the best actions you can use as a strategy to achieve your goals? We use the One Page Plan with Goal Boss - it is the result of boiling down a bigger strategic plan into a simple, actionable one-sheet that you can show to everyone and anyone. Below is a sample One Page Plan for reference.

The one page plan is made up of only five things. Vision, Mission, Values, Big Five Goals, and Big Five Strategies. Let's walk through those at a high level, and then dig a little bit deeper into each.

Vision

The first part of the one page plan is the vision. If your organization does not have a vision statement, you need develop one. What is a vision statement? A vision statement is your idea of what the world looks like because you and your organization exist. What does your perfect world look like? Whatever it is that you do to make the world a better place, that's your vision statement. A vision statement is the rock on which your house is built. That is the "why" behind what you do. What happens in your perfect world? How does that look? You need to describe that. Not just for yourself, but for your teammates and your customers.

Vision statements can and should be lofty. Reach for the stars. It is fine if your vision of the world is outside your grasp. Our vision at Goal Boss is a world where all teams are high performing teams and can accomplish anything. We know it is not likely all teams will get there. But that doesn't stop us from imagining the world that way. The vision inspires us. It keeps us positive when the going gets tough. Since leadership is about inspiration, reaching for things beyond your grasp helps you grow. It is the way you push yourself and your teams forward.

Mission

Your mission statement is about how you are going to achieve your vision. What does your organization do to realize the vision? The vision is the dream. The mission is the action. Your mission statement should be straightforward and easy to understand. It should also be easy to check up on. Here's an example.

The mission statement at Goal Boss is *To share and implement the Goal Boss Leadership System at every opportunity.* Simple. Wherever there is a team, or a member of a team, we work to share and implement Goal Boss. We do this because it is our deeply held belief that a world where all teams are high performing teams would be a significantly better place than the world we live in today. Our mission supports our vision. Yours can as well.

A mission statement is easy to check on. As a member of the team, do your actions support the mission? Will the things you are doing and saying right now increase the chances you will achieve your mission, which in turn will help your organization realize its vision? If you do not have a mission statement, develop one!

Values

What are the values you as an organization hold dear? What should others notice when they observe your behaviors? Where does your passion and drive come from? What behaviors do you exhibit as an organization? Pick 5 values that clearly define who you are.

At Goal Boss, our values are Teamwork, Hard Work, Communication, Delegation and Time Management. These are our values because in our experience, people whose behavior supports these values are often high performing members of high performing teams.

Organizations with written, shared values are more likely to achieve their goals and succeed. Why? Because written values provide the entire team with a sanity check of sorts. At any moment, you can ask yourself, or a teammate - Is the task you are doing right now aligned with one or more of your values? If so, do more of that. If not, stop doing what you're doing and reset.

Big Five Goals

As an organization what do you want to accomplish, no matter what? What are your big five goals for this year? That is what you want to show in your One Page Plan. What are your big five goals for this year that you intend to accomplish, no matter what?

The Big Five Goals bring focus and purpose to everyone in the organization. They help to ground the team in a way that makes the organization's vision, mission and values tangible. Everyone likes to fantasize about how it feels to be rich and famous. To have the big house. The fancy car. The amazing vacations. What you need for that is a vision. Without a mission, the vision cannot come true. Without values, the mission comes apart. Without the Big Five Goals, you run the risk of getting mired in the day to day. You need your Big Five Goals to ensure that everything you do this month, or this week, or today is moving you closer to achieving your mission.

Big Five Strategies

Strategies are just that. For each of your goals, create a simple, straightforward strategy to direct how you will achieve your Big Five Goals. How are you going to get this work done? What are the big strategies you are going to deploy to make sure your goals happen no matter what? Strategies are practical and tactical. Maybe you didn't know the goal. But, even if that were so, you could follow the strategies and still move the organization closer to its goals. But please, make sure everyone knows the goals.

Sample One Page Plan

At the risk of repeating myself, below is a review of our sample One Page Plan. It is a sample plan, but feel free to adopt parts of it, and make changes to fit your organization.

Vision • Mission • Values

We inspire high-performing teams to accomplish anything. That is what we picture when we close our eyes here at Goal Boss and think about the world. We inspire high-performing teams to accomplish anything. There is nothing that a Goal Boss client cannot accomplish. There is nothing you cannot accomplish now that you have this book. That is our vision.

Our mission is to share and implement the Goal Boss Leadership System at every opportunity. If you get in the car with me, if we are riding on a train, if we are hanging out at a coffee house, and you don't know I work with Goal Boss, you are going to find out! I am going to find out what kind of organization you work with. I am going to see if there is opportunity for us to implement the Goal Boss System in your organization. I know if I do that, I can inspire your high-performing team to accomplish anything. That is our mission.

Teamwork, hard work, communication, delegation, and time management are our values. If you are working at Goal Boss whatever you do as member of the Goal Boss organization should support one or more of our values. Teamwork, hard work, communication, delegation and time management are the behaviors we value most. Those are our core values. If you ever see me doing something that does not exemplify at least one of those values, please give me feedback about it right away. I do not want to be an example of anything but the very best my organization has to offer.

Written and shared vision, mission, and values are absolutely critical to an organization. Everything else is untethered without vision, mission, and values.

The vision, mission, and values in this example are the actual vision, mission and values of Goal Boss. The rest of the sample One Page Plan shows an imaginary company called Joe's Screen Doors. This is just a sample of information to give you an idea of the things you may want to put in your One Page Plan.

Big Five Goals

Goal Number One for the year: Sign forty major accounts. Here at Joe's Screen Doors, we have some major accounts at present and for Goal number one want forty more of them. Goal number two: Twenty million dollars in gross revenue. Goal Number Three: Greater than twenty-five percent gross margin. Goal Number Four: Overtime hours, less than five percent. Goal Number Five: Five hundred thousand daily average users of our mobile app.

Big Five Strategies

Our Big Five Strategies are designed to help us achieve the goals, no matter what. When you write yours, try to line them up so that your strategy number one matches your goal number one, and that strategy number two matches your second goal, etc. The One Page Plan is supposed to be simple and concise.

Business development strategy. Supercharge communication between marketing, sales and service teams. Clearly define the sales process, key metrics, goals and action steps to assigning clear ownership and reporting structured individual action plans for all account reps.

The next big strategy is focused on customer service. We will integrate customer support systems with inbound marketing and business systems. We will refine our customer service key metrics to identify trends. We will commission independent customer satisfaction surveys and user experience testing.

Strategy Number Three is about resource management. We will implement a team driven cost savings program to recognize and reward what we call ownership thinking. We will conduct cost-benefit analyses of the top twenty percent and the bottom twenty percent of the expense items so we can economize or eliminate redundant and unnecessary expenses.

Strategy Number Four is to develop our leaders. Goal Boss Leadership workshops for executives, directors and managers. We will implement Goal Boss teams across the organization from the top to the bottom. We are going to train our executives, directors and managers in one-on-one coaching so they can coach their direct reports and improve productivity from their teams. We will implement Rapid Values Onboarding™ for all new employees so they can get up to speed faster, and we are going implement periodic 360 feedback for all executives, directors and managers.

Strategy Number Five is to generate awareness and interest in our products by creating compelling, relevant, optimized content for potential customers. We are going to build and grow a world-class marketing automation system that serves as a force multiplier for our sales team.

That is the entire one page plan. The One Page Plan is a quick summary of the detailed strategic plan for the year. But even your full-blast strategic plan for the year does not need to be one of those two-hundred-page, fancy consulting firm documents that you pay five or six figures for and then put on a shelf because it is so big and complicated that no one can understand it or has time to read it.

A strategic plan should be a simple and straightforward. A document that anyone can understand. The One Page Plan is literally one page. Keep it on your desk. It can stay as your computer desktop. You can print it as a poster and hang it in the break room. Everyone in the organization can see it because nothing on the document is confidential.

With everyone in the organization on the same page, you begin to get your organization aligned. When you run into problems, and you will, remember what Eisenhower told us: Planning is indispensable.

The most important thing the One Page Plan does is clearly communicate to the entire organization who you are, why you're here and where you're going.

Key Takeaways

In the space below, write your Key Takeaways from this chapter.

_____

_____

_____

_____

_____

_____

_____

_____

_____

_____

_____

_____

_____

_____

one page plan - joe's screen doors

Vision	We inspire high performing teams to accomplish anything.
Mission	To share and implement the goal boss leadership system at every opportunity.

Values

1. Teamwork	2. Hard Work	3. Communication	4. Delegation	5. Time Management

Big 5 Goals for 2017

1. Sign 40 Major Accounts	2. $20M Gross Revenue	3. >25% Gross Margin	4. Overtime Hours <5%	5. 500,000 DAU's

Big 5 Strategies To Achieve Our Goals

1. Business Development	2. Customer Service	3. Resource Management	4. Develop Our Leaders	5. Inbound Marketing
Supercharge communication between marketing, bizdev, sales and service teams.	Integrate customer support systems with inbound marketing and bizdev systems.	Implement team-driven cost savings program to recognize and reward "Ownership Thinking".	Goal Boss Leadership workshops for execs, directors, and managers.	Generate awareness and interest in our products by creating compelling, relevant, optimized content for potential customers.
Clearly define the sales process, key metrics, goals and action steps, assigning clear ownership and reporting structure. Individual action plans for all account representatives.	Refine customer service key metrics to identify trends. Commission independent customer satisfaction survey and user experience testing.	Conduct cost-benefit analysis on top 20% and bottom 20% of expense items to economize or eliminate the redundant and unnecessary.	Implement Goal Boss Teams. Train execs, directors and managers in 1-on-1 Coaching for their direct-reports. Implement 90 day onboarding plans for all new employees, and 360 feedback for execs, directors and managers.	Build and grow a world-class marketing automation system that serves as a force multiplier for our sales team.

CHAPTER FIFTEEN

Keys to Planning

N ow we know the value of a plan and we know what makes a proper goal. Let's go through the keys to planning. That will give us an overview of the details involved. We have carefully distilled planning to make the process straightforward for you and your organization.

Alignment

The first key to planning is alignment. Make sure that everyone on the team and that everyone in the organization knows the plan, and the reason the organization exists.

Vision • Mission • Values

Communicate your vision, mission, and values across the entire organization. Make no secret of these. Everyone in your organization should know your vision, mission, and values. They could even be memorized as part of every ninety-day onboarding plan.

Five Year Vision

High performing organizations looking to the future need a Five-Year Vision. Make certain you have a clear picture of what your world would look like five years from now, and share that vision with everyone in the organization. Everyone on the team needs to know where you are going.

One Page Plan

Once each year invest a day or two and update your five-year vision. Maybe it will look exactly like that in five years, and maybe not. Probably not. A one year tactical plan - a One Page Plan - is absolutely necessary. This tells your team exactly where you are going this year. Reviewing the One Page Plan is how you check to make sure what you are doing right now is moving you in the direction you need to go as a team and as an organization.

Organizational Communication Plan

Every high performing team needs an organizational communication plan. This plan describes how you communicate with one another and what methods of communication are acceptable. What are the rules of engagement in regard to email? Instant messaging? Social media? How do you communicate with one another as an organization? Don't leave this to chance, work with your team to decide what you want, then manage and lead to that standard.

Planning Questions

When considering a planning session, whether a one-page plan, or a five-year plan, you want to look for answers to a number of common planning questions. If you answer these, you can put together a plan.

- Where have you been? It is a simple concept and often overlooked, but examining your past performance is necessary to understanding your organization.
- Where are you now? Taking stock of your current situation will help you understand how successful past actions and strategies were, or weren't!
- Where are you going?
- What is the vision of the future?
    o What is your five-year vision?
    o What is your one year vision?
- Where do you want to go with this organization?
- How will you get there?
- What are your strategies to achieve your goals?
- Who do you need to help you execute on these strategies?
- What people do you already have that you need?
- Are there any people you need that you don't have right now? Let's figure out who is going to help you get to your goal.
- When will you arrive?
- Again, one year goals, five year goals, and perhaps even ten-year goals. But absolutely one year goals and five-year goals.

Planning Process

The Goal Boss planning process is simple and effective. It is designed to make sure that the right people are involved from start to finish, and to ensure every member of the team takes ownership of the plan. Few things are less inspiring than being handed a document and told, "Here is the plan. Go do it." Remember for a plan to succeed, the team must be involved. This process will get you and your team to the finish line.

Who's on the Team?

If you are the leader of the team figure out what your goals are, then select the people you need to achieve those goals. These are the people who will to be on your team, the people you cannot do without.

Use A Facilitator

When you conduct your planning process, particularly as the leader of the team, hire a facilitator to help you run the meeting. This practice frees you to bring your vision, your mission, and your values to the team. Planning an important strategy session and leading it are two separate efforts. As the leader, you must be free to communicate effectively with your team and drive performance in the planning session. Get a facilitator.

Gather Pre-Planning Surveys

Prior to your planning session you can send out a strategic planning survey. The survey asks all the questions you want answered in the meeting. You do not need to start from scratch in your planning session. You can gather everyone's individual answers to the pre-planning survey, collate all of them, and then as a team you can identify the best thinking of the group. It is an amazingly efficient way to get everyone's best ideas and everyone's best thinking available to the meeting before the meeting ever starts. Better still, ask your professional facilitator to do it for you. A professional facilitator can have the surveys ready to go within a few minutes.

Conduct the Planning Session

When you conduct a planning session, make sure you find a fresh environment. A comfortable meeting room, a resort, or a hotel. Get off campus if you can. Turn off your phones. This is where you are going to lay the groundwork for the next year of your success. Do not shortchange yourself by trying to do this quickly, or in a noisy, distracted environment. Give yourself the time, the space, and the focus necessary to create an amazing strategic plan.

Review and Revise the Draft Plan

When the planning session is done, the facilitator will create a draft plan for distribution to your team. The team can then give feedback once again to make sure you have it absolutely right.

Finalize and Distribute the Plan.

When final review is complete, your facilitator will finalize and distribute the plan in two different versions. There will be the detailed strategic plan that the executive team and the leadership of the organization will see, and there will be the One Page Plan, which will be scrubbed of confidential information so it can be distributed across the entire organization. When all is said and done, everyone in the organization will have access to a straightforward, actionable, written plan. Everyone on your team will know where you are going, how you will get there, and how they can contribute.

Use Goal Boss

The Goal Boss Platform is built specifically for executing on your plan. If you prefer another management system, then use it. The important thing is that you do have a system and a process to lead and manage your organization and your teams.

Key Metrics

Use key metrics to recognize and measure what is important and to identify action steps. Make sure you keep moving things in the right direction.

Goal Boss Teams

Goal Boss Teams are specialized groups within the organization who take ownership of specific Key Metrics and organizational initiatives. Teams following this process help ensure everyone in the organization knows what they can do to be most useful. This helps everyone on the team to grow both personally and professionally. That growth, in turn, drives results and performance for the entire organization.

Thirty Day Goals

Everyone on a Goal Boss team has between three and seven 30-day goals that are narrow in scope, focused, and important to the overall plan. Thirty-day goals across the entire organization make the difference between an ordinary company and a high performing team.

Team Problem Solving

Team Problem Solving helps you kick the big problems out of the way so you can keep moving forward. It is how you solve problems in ten minutes rather than talking about them for thirty or forty minutes with no real results. Use team problem solving to get things done so you can keep moving the needle on your key metrics and make your plans come true.

Those are the keys to planning. If you follow these simple steps your record of successes will to increase drastically. So, follow the steps!

Key Takeaways

In the space below, write your Key Takeaways from this chapter.

_____

_____

_____

_____

_____

_____

_____

_____

_____

_____

_____

_____

_____

KEYS TO PLANNING

Alignment
* Vision, Mission, Values
* Five Year Vision
* One Year Tactical Plan (One Page Plan)
* Organizational Communication Plan

Planning Questions
* Where have we been?
* Where are we now?
* Where are we going?
* How do we get there?
* Who do we need?
* When will we arrive?

Planning Process
* Who's on the team?
* Use a facilitator to maximize team performance
* Gather pre-planning surveys
* Conduct the planning session
* Review and revise draft plan
* Finalize and distribute the plan

Use Goal Boss
* Key Metrics
* Goal Boss Teams
* 30-Day Goals
* Team Problem Solving

goal boss

CHAPTER SIXTEEN

Organizing Resources

Winnie the Pooh author A.A. Milne wrote, "Organizing is what you do before you do something so that when you do it, it's not all mixed up." I am not sure even Shakespeare could put it better than that. Let's look at Organizing so the next time you do something, it's not all mixed up!

Managing Resources

The definition of organizing is to align resources for maximum achievement. You must align and organize your resources to achieve your goals. We have covered goals thoroughly. Now we will take a close look at resources to define what they are and how they work. Resources fall into three main categories. Time, people, and money.

The first and most important is time. Time is the only thing you can't get more of. All we know for certain is you and I are both going to run out of time eventually. Treat time as the precious, irreplaceable, totally unique resource that it is. You cannot get more time.

People are the second of the big three resources. People are precious, amazing, unique. People need care, recognition, attention and development in order to thrive. How you organize, manage and lead people is almost as important is how you organize and manage your time.

The third big resource is money. We are not going to go into detail about money and finance in this book. How that works is another conversation. That being said, how you organize around the availability of money as a resource is critically important.

Time and the OOTO

Once upon a time, there were three brothers. Matt, Mike and Mark. These three brothers opened up a flower shop in the city. They all knew how to work hard and they all had big dreams. They also had an assistant named Sarah, and they had a van. Other than themselves and the van, they didn't have much. Theirs was a bootstrapped startup the purest form.

Because there was only one van, whenever Matt had to deliver flowers to a customer, he would send an email with the subject line "OOTO" to Mike, Mark and Sara. OOTO stands for Out of The Office. When Matt needed to run a delivery, he would send the email to three people letting them know that he had the van would be back later. This was an effective way of keeping the team advised about his progress. But let's do the resource math on that process, just to be sure.

One email goes out to three people, which takes about a minute apiece. One minute for Matt to write and send the email, plus three minutes total for Mike, Mark and Sarah to read the email, equals four minutes total. Matt would make around three deliveries a day. So, the team spent roughly twelve minutes every day on Matts OOTO emails. In the context of a small startup business where the team has a fair bit of downtime, that is probably a pretty good investment of those twelve minutes a day. Or is it?

Think about this twelve minutes a day, five days a week, for fifty weeks a year. That comes to three thousand minutes a year, also known as fifty hours. From the early days of their business, Matt's OOTO email was eating up one full week of employee time for writing and reading the same email over and over again. Remember, this was a startup. They were hard working, and they needed to know where the van and one another were at all times.

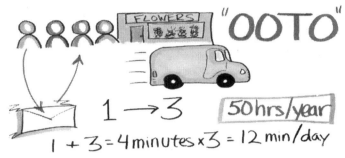

On the surface, the OOTO emails looked like a passable way to manage their human and equipment resources. OOTO was one of many tactics the brothers used in their business. "It just works," Matt would say. OOTO let everybody know where the important resources of the organization were. This basic communication strategy helped them achieve their goals each and every day.

In time, the company grew to dozens of vans, hundreds of employees, and thousands of customers. And even though Matt was not doing the deliveries himself anymore, whenever he left the office for any reason, he would send out an OOTO email to everyone in the company. Just like back in the day, it took Matt about a minute to write and send the OOTO email. Just like back in the day, it took employees about a minute each to read the email. Just like back in the day, Matt would leave the office about three times a day. So, every single day, over nine hundred minutes of productivity were spent making sure everyone knew when Matt was leaving the office and when he would be back.

Do the math! Nine hundred minutes is just over fifteen hours. Every single day, Matt was paying his employees to spend fifteen hours reading the same email over and over again. Almost two full time salaries were being spent just so everyone in the company knew Matt was out of the office. Because Matt was the leader of the company, people would read his emails. People would also emulate his behaviors. So, here was a service business with hundreds of employees coming and going all day, every day, and broadcasting OOTOs at an amazing rate. Thousands of hours, and hundreds of thousands of payroll dollars were being wasted every year by the OOTO. What is the key takeaway?

Time is the only thing you can't get more of. There is no such thing as a little bit of time. A few minutes a day, just 10 minutes a day, adds up to forty-one hours a year. There is no such thing as a little bit of time, because time is the only resource you can't get more of.

Beware the OBT

Let's look at how people, one of the big three resources, behave in the workplace. Specifically, we are going to look at two important attributes. We can demonstrate it by building a little a little X/Y graph.

On the x-axis (the horizontal one), is a representation of values. Values are the beliefs and attitudes that the company seeks in exemplary employees. What do they think about the company? Do they sing the company song? Do they like to go to the company picnic and participate in its events? How do they feel about being part of the

PERFORMANCE (SKILLS)

VALUES (ATTITUDE)

organization? Do their values fit with those of the organization? On the y-axis of the graph, we see performance. Skills. How good is a person at her job? That's what we are looking at. Values and performance. Said differently, attitude and skills.

Graph every single person in your organization based on these two criteria. We are going to look at the different quadrants on this graph and see if we can draw some conclusions that will help you assess the level of performance, engagement, and success, in your organization.

Let's start with our best-case scenario, in the top right corner of your graph. This area is for one of your team members who has great performance. They are way up on the performance scale, and they have excellent values. They love the company and they do a  great job. The whole team loves to see that person at work. Maybe you are that person at work. I work extremely hard to be that person at work.

That person is your A-Player. Your superstar. They kind, generous, an effective leader, they do great work every day.

In terms of values and performance, this is your goal for everyone in the organization. Everybody on the team. You want A-Players. Now, let's look at somebody who's good at their job and who embodies company values pretty well. In terms of both performance and values they are slightly above average. Not someone to worry about but not setting the world on fire either.

This is your B-Player. What is the goal with a B-player? If you are the leader of this B-player, what is your goal for them? Where do you want this person to go? I ask this question every time we do a workshop, every time we do an event, every time I coach leaders, I ask what is the

goal for the B player? The answer I get every time is, "My goal for the B-player is to turn them into an A-player." That is the right answer.

Leaders and HR professionals routinely take steps to make that happen. They coach that person, they train that person, they give the B-player encouragement and resources. Maybe they have teamed them with one of the A-players to help develop the B-players into A-players.

The goal for the B-player is to turn them into an A-player, which makes all the sense in the world.

Next, let's look at somebody who truly loves your company. Somebody who's been with your company for a long time. They started when it was little and they have been here every day since. They have been singing the company song, planning the picnic, doing all of the things that somebody who really loves an organization would do. Sadly, they haven't really grown with the organization at the same pace. Maybe they are just not very good at their job. They absolutely exemplify the corporate values. They wear the jacket and the shirt. Deeply engaged in the values of the company. But, their performance is not particularly good. They don't do good work. They are just hanging on. So, we call this person the hanger-oner. Most organizations have at least one.

What's the danger of the hanger-oner? They are pleasant, everyone likes to be around them, and they love the organization. The danger is this: as long as the rest of your team does a little bit better work than the hanger-oner, they are protected. All someone has to do to not get fired is keep their performance be a little bit better than a hanger-oner. Then, if you are their boss and you say "Well you know, your performance is really low, we are thinking of letting you go. All they have to do is say: "What about the Hanger-oner? They do a much worse job than I do." Even if their values aren't way up there like the hanger-oner, if their performance is just a little bit better, they feel protected.

The hanger-oner sets the minimum acceptable standard for performance, and that's a truly dangerous thing because high performing organizations need minimum performance at the B-level or above.

Let's look at someone who scores high in the performance category, but low on values. Here is someone in your organization who is incredibly good at what they do. They are highly skilled and the numbers prove it. For our example, this could be a salesperson. They do an amazingly good job all the time. This is your rainmaker. The problem is that this person does not exemplify the values of your company. Put simply, they have got an attitude problem. They poison the well, and have bad things to say about the organization. After our sample salesperson hits the quota in the middle of the month, they put their feet up on the desk and wonder out loud why everybody around them is such a jerk. They bring arrogance and discord to the team. They get a whole lot done but they torture everybody around them and foster a toxic environment. I am sure as I describe this person, you can probably think of their name.

Say hello to your Onboard Terrorist, or OBT. Terrorist is a strong word. I use that term because it's accurate. This is important. Just like the hanger-oner who sets the bar for minimum acceptable performance, the OBT sets the minimum acceptable standard for values. In this model, all an employee has to do to remain in the organization is to be a little bit less of a jerk than the OBT, and a little bit less of a failure than the hanger-oner. Survival in this organization sits just to the right and above the intersection of the Hanger-oner and the OBT's values and performance measurements.

The Hanger-oner and the OBT are truly dangerous to your organization and that's why I strongly suggest that you graph everybody in your organization in terms of their performance and their values. Rate everyone from one to ten on both of these metrics. It might be a bit subjective, especially on the values scale. On the performance scale, it should be more measurable. The better you get at using the Goal Boss System, the more and more measurable both metrics will be. But, if you graph everybody in the organization based simply on your assessment of their performance and their values, you will know where you stand and you will also be able to give your teammates the tools they need to improve in terms of both their values and their performance.

An important question that we get asked all the time is, "How on Earth did we get ourselves an OBT in the first place? Where did our onboard terrorists come from?"

The answer to the question is often more puzzling and upsetting than you would expect. The fact of the matter is that we tend to grow our own onboard terrorists. We bring it on ourselves. Remember how the B player is identified and then given training, focus, attention, and love to turn them into an A-player? When that happens, when the B-player is finally transformed into an A-player, the newly minted A-player usually doesn't get the continued attention that they have gotten used to. As an A-player begins to perform, you'll probably recognize a different B-player, then focus your efforts and energy on them. That's when the A-player stays up at the top of the performance graph, but starts to slip to the left side of the values metric. They think to themselves "I used to go out to lunch with my boss at least once a month. I used to get all this love and now I don't. This isn't as great a place to work as I thought it was. It was really great for a while but it's less great than it used to be and I'm doing a great job. I've gotten all of these skills but they are focusing on that other guy now and I don't get the recognized anymore. Am I just doing it for the money? You know what, this place kind of sucks and I think I'm going to share that with everybody else in the organization because if somebody who is as awesome as me cannot be happy in a place like this, I need to let everybody know that!"

Boom. Your very own, homegrown OBT.

If you have got somebody in your organization who's been there for a long time and they answer to the description of the onboard terrorist, that might be on you. Letting the onboard terrorist go, firing the onboard terrorist, moving them on, is one of the hardest decisions that you'll ever make as a leader, because usually there's a significant financial cost that comes along with letting this person go. They do such incredibly great work, so we are afraid to let them go. But you know what? In my experience, and every situation is different and so you want to manage this carefully, I have found that the cost of keeping the onboard terrorist, even though they are the highest performing member of your team, the cost to the morale and productivity of everyone else in the organization is extraordinarily high. Think about that.

Same goes for the hanger-oner. People will often wonder, "Why is so-and-so still working here? They don't do great work. Yeah, they are nice and all. But I work hard and I'm just as nice!"

Keeping people on the fringes of acceptable behavior and performance widens the range of acceptable behavior and performance, when what you want as a leader is a team of A-players and B-players.

Last, and least, is the easiest part of this whole model. The employee with poor values and low performance. They are not very good at their job and they don't exemplify the values of the company. That's the C-player and that's the easiest decision you make as a leader, right?

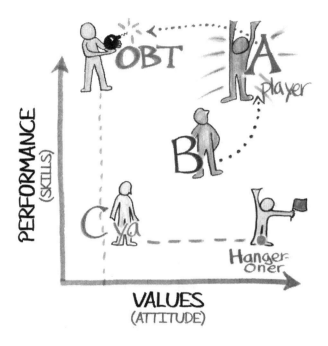

The reason we look at values and performance so carefully, and the reason that I am so passionate about this particular issue is that the goal of any high-performing organization is to make sure that we've got B-players at the very least and we are always working to develop them into A-player's. That's what a high-performing team looks like.

T.A.S.K.

An important key to organizing is staffing. Finding, hiring and keeping the right people. How do we achieve that? People are one of the big three key resources. Unlike any other resource, people are complex. People need to learn, grow and change in order to find meaning in their lives. Leadership is about helping people find meaning and purpose in their roles. The goal of resource management is to make the organization as productive as possible. Where people are concerned, this requires a workforce who, for lack of a better term, love what they do. There's an acronym known as T.A.S.K. which is highly instructive in this regard. T.A.S.K. stands for Talent, Attitude, Skills, Knowledge. Let's walk through them one at a time.

Talent

The first thing we want to talk about is talent. The dictionary defines talent as the natural endowments of a person. Talent is one of those traits you know when you see. If somebody has great eye-hand coordination, or they are super quick at thinking on their feet, or are really great with people, or they are excellent at solving complex problems, we say they have talent. Great artists and athletes are usually born with talents that they later develop. We know talent when we see it. It is important to gauge and assess the talent of an individual when you're thinking about bringing them into the organization, or adding them to your team. The key thing to keep in mind about talent is that talent is there, or it's not. People are born with talent, or they are not.

Attitude

"A" stands for Attitude. We all have an attitude and our attitudes tend to change with mood or circumstance. That being said, you still can kind of get a feel for a person's overall attitude, and you should. Are they generally a positive person? Are they curious? Are they negative? Are they sarcastic? Are they generous and kind? What is the attitude that you see? Because a person's attitude is prevalent all the time and people tend to have overriding attitudes. It's important to understand how attitude figures into staffing.

Skills

Skills are the things you and I know how to do. Straight up. Things you have learned. Perhaps you can ride a bicycle, or fly an airplane, or lead a seminar. Maybe you can build a house. Skills are things people have gone about the process of learning. The difference between talent and skill is that you can learn how to do a skill.

Knowledge

Knowledge is the information you have. The things you know. Through study and experience, people gather knowledge. You gain knowledge from formal education, books, seminars and workshops, and from life experience. Mistakes bring knowledge, as do successes. And so, we gain knowledge over time. Knowledge is something that we are always building, and we'll always have. Best of all when it comes to knowledge, if you don't know something, you can learn it.

Joe's Tire Shop

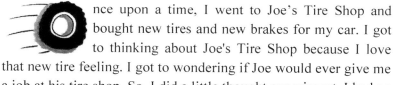 nce upon a time, I went to Joe's Tire Shop and bought new tires and new brakes for my car. I got to thinking about Joe's Tire Shop because I love that new tire feeling. I got to wondering if Joe would ever give me a job at his tire shop. So, I did a little thought experiment. I had an imaginary interview with Joe at the tire store. Here's how it went.

I said "Hey, Joe. Would you hire me at your tire store, or could I interview for the job at least?" Since I'm a good customer Joe might give me the interview just to be polite. So, we got started on the interview right away.

Joe started by doing an assessment of me. He wanted to know things about me. Joe asked, "So Will, do you have any experience? Do you know how to operate a tire machine?"

I answered, "No, Joe. I don't know how to operate a tire machine. I don't have that skill."

"Okay," Joe replied, "Have you ever worked the point-of-sale system? That cash register here at our tire shop?"

"Honestly Joe, I haven't," I said. "I've never operated a point-of-sale system. I don't know how to do that. I don't have that skill either."

Joe remained patient, and said, "When you come here, we size the tires on your car. There's three numbers that determine the size, type and quality of tire. Are you familiar with how the tire sizing system works?"

"No, Joe. As a matter fact, I don't have knowledge of the tire sizing system yet." I answered. By now, I could see that Joe was less certain than ever that I'd be a good employee for his tire store. But, as a great guy and a professional, he pressed on.

"Let's talk about experience. Do you have any experience selling tires in a tire store? Have you ever done that before," Joe inquired.

"No, I haven't Joe. I don't have any experience selling tires," I admitted happily.

At this point it wasn't looking so good for me, right? I clearly lacked the skills and knowledge that I would need to be successful in the tire business. But, Joe is a good guy and he's wanting to throw me a bone. He's doing the best he can to figure out whether or not I could fit into his organization. Joe is trying, and so am I.

Joe says: "You've definitely got some gaps in terms of the skills and knowledge required to work here, Will. May I ask what reasons you think there are that maybe we should hire you into the organization?"

In my thought experiment interview, I said, "I don't have the skills and knowledge that we talked about, Joe. But I have built several roller coasters in my backyard. I designed and machined the parts and the track and the cart myself. So, I've definitely got talent. I'm mechanically inclined, absolutely. I'm really good with people, and with sales. You can see that just by the fact that we are having this conversation. I know you're trying hard to find a way to get me into the organization, or give me a chance, and I'm grateful for that. I like to think that's because I'm really good at connecting with people. I've got good empathy. So, even though I don't know how to sell tires yet, I can learn about that and use my people skills to become one of your top salespeople.

Like I said, I'm mechanically inclined. I know how to build just about anything. I can take stuff apart and put it back together. I'm really good at problem-solving. I've been a certified flight instructor and I've been a commercial pilot. One of the things that I learned in my piloting was the importance of safety, and the importance of being careful around big machines. In a shop like yours where things can go wrong in a hurry, it's important to be careful. Safety starts with the right attitude. You won't have to teach me that, Joe!"

Joe is listening, intently. So, I continue, "I just love the tire industry. I read about tires. I see all the magazines. I know about the different manufacturers. So again, I'm a big fan of the tire industry. Another thing I believe in is loyalty. I bring a real sense of teamwork and loyalty to the team. As a matter fact, if you look at my resume, you'll see that I stay at a job for 5 years. Sometimes I've stayed longer, but at least five years. That's my track record. I really do like to think that I bring something to the table here even though I don't have the skills knowledge that we were talking about before. Correction. I don't have those skills and knowledge... yet!"

I might say those things to Joe if I was trying to get a job doing something I'd never done before. What is Joe going to think at this point? Its possible Joe might say, "Yeah, you don't know how to work tire machine and we are done." He could say that, it happens all the time in job interview situations. When we are thinking about bringing somebody on to the team, we tend to ask the question, "Have you ever done this before?" and if no then no. That is a mistake.

It's a mistake because talent and attitude are the things in a person that are just baked in. There's nothing you can do to add talent or improve attitude if it's not already there. Clearly, I can learn how to use that tire machine. I've got the talent to do this job. I've got the attitude that he needs on the sales floor and in the shop. I'm great with people and I understand about safety and I understand about process. I'm the guy that you'd want if only I knew how to do the job.

Skills and knowledge can absolutely be taught. You cannot often teach talent or attitude, but you can teach me how to work a tire machine and you can teach me how to run the POS system. I can learn the tire sizing system and I can sell tires because I have sold other things. It's just a matter of me getting that new experience. So, what is the takeaway once we know that talent and attitude are baked in and people basically got it or they don't, while skills and knowledge can be taught? If someone doesn't have a skill, they can learn it. Especially if they have got talent and a positive attitude.

When you are hiring, when you are growing your team, hire for talent and attitude and train for skills and knowledge.

Key Takeaways

In the space below, write your Key Takeaways from this chapter.

_____

_____

_____

_____

_____

_____

_____

_____

_____

_____

_____

_____

_____

CHAPTER SEVENTEEN

Successful Delegation

In the 3rd century B.C. there lived a man named Archimedes. Archimedes was a mathematician, a scientist, an engineer, philosopher and a botanist.

He said, "Give me a lever and a place to stand and I shall move the Earth with it." Archimedes was talking about leverage and along the way he defined the mathematics of leverage. He understood the art and science of applying a very small amount of energy through a well-built system and doing an amazing amount of work. Does that sound familiar? *Give me a place to stand and I shall move the earth.* In our environment, we are talking about delegation.

As a skill, delegation lives at the intersection of expert time management and inspired leadership. You will not become a successful leader without it. Let's go through the steps to successful delegation. When you do the all steps of delegation properly and in order, you will get things done. On the other hand, if you skip any of these steps, you may never master the skill of delegation.

Delegation is another one of Big Three Career Killers. To recap, the career killers are Communication, Delegation, and Time Management. Both delegation and time management are parts of Organizing. When you reach the limit of your delegation skills, when you're not able to delegate any more tasks in your career, that is where your career stops. You must learn to get more and more done without doing those things yourself if you want to grow as a leader. You must learn to delegate! I cannot overstate this!

There is no reward in business, or in life, for doing things yourself. The old saying if you want something done right, do it yourself is utter nonsense. That is something a poor manager would say. It is not something a great leader would say. Get things done without doing things yourself. That is delegation. Don't just do it, just get it done. Without further ado, here are the Steps to Successful Delegation

Know the Goal

Start by knowing what your goal is. Perform expert goal setting before you delegate a task. Write SMART goals and be sure Goal Certainty is in the range of eighty percent.

Choose the Right Person

Figure out who's got the resources, the talent, the skills, the time, the energy, and the passion, to get this thing done. There is one person who is the right person for this task. Choose one, and only one person for the task.

Share the Background and Facts

Describe how you got to this point, what the goal is, what are the issues, and the reason why this goal is important. What is it that we want to achieve with this goal? Make sure you share that information with the right person so that they can bring the same amount of passion, integrity, and ownership that you are bringing to the goal.

Clearly Define Results

If you know the goal and you have written a smart goal in the first place, you should have a pretty good idea of what success will look like. Make sure you clearly define success and share that definition of success with the person you are delegating to. Don't leave anything to chance.

Encourage Feedback & Questions

After you have clearly defined success, stop talking and listen. Get feedback and questions from the person you are delegating to. Give them every opportunity to clarify. Use the communication loop. Make sure that they play the goal back to you. That way, you will know you did a good job of communicating it in the first place. If there is misunderstanding, start over, instead of hoping for the best.

Set Clear Deadlines

Make sure that you know what the deadline is and make sure that the person you're delegating to knows what the deadline is. Say the deadline out loud and ask them to say it back to you. A task without a deadline is due… never!

Give the Whole Job to One Person

The easiest way to spot a weak leader is if they give a goal to several people and expect them to figure out who is in charge. It is disrespectful and inefficient. Don't assign a task or goal to multiple people. Make sure there is one owner of this goal, one owner of this result. They may get help from other people, but they are the one you are talking to, they are the one who owns this, they are the one who is responsible. Don't spread it out because then you may well get he-said-she-said nonsense, and "I thought you were doing it," excuses. When nobody is in charge, everybody is in charge. High performing organizations don't do that. High performing organizations assign a task to a person.

Provide All the Necessary Resources

Ask, "Is there anything you need to get this done?" Take the time to discuss the goal and be certain that the person you are delegating to has the tools, authority, time, and any other resources they will need to be successful.

Offer Guidance Without Micromanaging

Don't step in halfway through just because you think you can do a better job, or because you are unsure of where things stand. Trust the person you have delegated to. Let them handle the goal from end to end. Let them manage through this process themselves. If you step in and take over, you erode that person's trust and confidence, you waste your own time, and you damage your standing as a leader. Offer guidance without micromanaging. When you offer guidance, do it by only asking questions if possible. People tend to know the right thing to do if you ask them the right questions and guide them.

Set SMART Goals

Make sure your goal is Specific, Measurable, Attainable, Relevant, and Time-bound. Without all these attributes, it is hard to know if a goal has been achieved. Don't set yourself or your team up for failure through ambiguity. Set SMART goals!

Follow Up

Following up is not the same thing as taking over. Remember: you are not micromanaging, you are not taking over. You are just checking in. Don't wait for the last minute. Don't live in hope. Hope is undiscovered disappointment. Follow up at set times from when you delegate to the time the goal is due so you know how it's going and so the person you delegated to knows that this is important.

Give Full Credit for Success

When a person succeeds in achieving the goal, give them one hundred percent of the credit. As the leader, you get zero percent. Imagine you get a thing done through delegation, and you deliver it to your board of directors and they say, "Hey, way to go!" That's when you say, "It wasn't me, it was Bill. I delegated that to Bill and he absolutely crushed it. He is an amazing player and we are lucky to have him on the team."

Take Full Responsibility for Failure

The flip side of giving credit for success is taking responsibility for failure. If you delegate this task to Bill and Bill doesn't come through, when the board asks, "Why isn't this done," you are not going to blame Bill. You are the leader. You take responsibility for any failure of the team. The players get credit for success, the leader takes responsibility for failure.

Those are the steps to successful delegation. You have to do them in this order, and you have to do them all. As a leader, you must master delegation. You must get better and better and better at delegating all the time. Because if you don't, your next boss will.

Key Takeaways

In the space below, write your Key Takeaways from this chapter.

_____

_____

_____

_____

_____

_____

_____

_____

_____

_____

_____

_____

_____

_____

SUCCESSFUL DELEGATION

Don't Just Do it, Just Get It Done!

1. Know the goal
2. Choose the right person
3. Share Background & Facts
4. Clearly Define Results
5. Encourage Feedback & Questions
6. Set Clear Deadlines
7. Give the whole job to one person
8. Provide all necessary resources
9. Offer guidance without micromanaging
10. Set SMART Goals
11. Follow-up
12. Give full credit to the person when they succeed
13. Take full responsibility for failure

"GIVE ME A LEVER AND

A PLACE TO STAND"...

~ ARCHIMEDES

 goal boss

CHAPTER EIGHTEEN

Keys to Organizing

Let's review the keys to organizing to make sure you manage your resources expertly. The better you get at organizing, the more successful and effective your leadership will become. Remember that two of the Big Three Career Killers are functions of organizing. Study these skills. Become a student of organizing.

Define and Communicate Goals

What's the Goal?

The first step in organizing is to define and communicate goals. The first question that we ask is, "What's the goal?" The goal must be clearly understood by you and your team, especially if you are the leader. There is no amount of clarity that is too much around the question of what's the goal.

Who's the Leader?

The second question we ask at the beginning of a meeting, a workshop, a seminar, a training, a road trip, or anything else worth doing is, "Who's the Leader?" There's an old saying that goes, "If nobody's in charge, everybody's in charge." This is a horrible way to run a team. There must be a named leader in order for organization to occur.

Identify Your Resources

Make sure that you know what your resources are, where they are, and who is managing them. Identify your resources and manage them accordingly.

Time • People • Money

The big three resources, as we've discussed, are time, people and money. There are several others that you're going to want to think about and talk about with your team.

Materials & Equipment

What are the materials that you need. How does your team forecast those requirements? How do you know what you're going to need and when you're going to need it? Among others, developing project management skills, enterprise resource planning skills, and financial management skills is absolutely crucial to running a well-organized company. Be certain that you know what equipment you have, what you will need, what the capacity of each piece of equipment is, and the lifespan of each piece of equipment. How are you going to capitalize those things? Stay ahead of the curve when it comes to materials and equipment. You don't want to be reactive. If you're the leader of a department, a division or an entire organization, consider delegating resource management by category as part of your leadership strategy.

Facilities and Technology

Make sure that the building, the office, the factory, whatever it is you need to run your organization, are suited to the purpose and also that you can afford those facilities and technology. Materials, equipment, facilities and technology are all assets. Chances are you're going to trade off cash or debt for those resources. Having a written facilities and technology plan at or before the start of every year is important to your strategic plan.

Education & Training

Managers ask, "What if we train our people and they leave?"

Leaders ask, "What if we don't train them and they stay?" Be a leader. Invest in your people. Every year, make sure your people have a detailed training and professional development plan and budget for that. Involve your people in the conversation. Ask your team members what they would like to learn and why? When someone makes a suggestion for their own training, they take ownership of the decision to learn to be responsible for the outcome.

Roles and Responsibilities

Going from your clearly defined set of Key Metrics, with ownership assigned to each, understanding and communicating roles and responsibilities should be uncomplicated. You should never struggle to answer the question, who does what?

Published Organization Chart

A published organization chart should be up to date and available to everyone. By up-to-date, I mean up to this particular date. Today. Every day the org chart should be up-to-date. Whenever there is a change, a revised org chart should be circulated throughout the organization. This is the best way to ensure that everyone in your organization knows Who's the leader. This ensures that everyone is clear on who's the leader of the entire organization and who's the leader in each department, division, and section of the company. Take time to ensure that everyone in organization understands the organization chart. Not just to answer the question of who's the leader, but also to give the entire organization an idea of what a career path might look like. One of your most important resources is people, and I promise you that anyone working in a company has at one time or another wondered what it might be like to have their boss's job, or the job after that, or the job after that. Publishing an organization chart serves that purpose as well.

Goal Boss Teams.

By reading this book, you are learning the entire Goal Boss Leadership System. You also have access to the Goal Boss website and the Goal Boss apps, and Goal Boss Certified Coaches if you so desire. Setting up Goal Boss Teams will help you drive accountability, get and measure results, engage with your direct reports and other departments, solve problems, and get stuff done at a rate most organizations only dream of. All high performing teams have a leadership system in place, and they use it.

Key Metrics

Measure what matters. As soon as you know what matters and you start to measure it, you will start to see changes in those areas. In the next chapter, you'll learn the details of how Key Metrics are measured and managed in the Goal Boss system.

Goals

Successful teams and leaders set goals. Make sure your goals and those of your team are SMART goals. Remember, the concept of Eulogy Goals. Will the goals set by you and your team really make a difference? Share your goals at the team level so everyone in the organization who needs to know, does know what you're working on. Shared goals allow other people in the organization to question your goals, to challenge your goals, to push you a little bit harder, and to make sure that if you need it, they are available and ready to lend a hand. A goal written is more likely to be achieved, and a goal shared across a team is even more likely than that.

Team Problem Solving

You already know that Team Problem Solving is a way of batch processing important, complicated conversations and surfacing the best action steps to solve those problems and get things done. Use the Goal Boss Leadership System in your organization and things will run more smoothly. It's been proven time and time again.

And that wraps it up for organizing. Remember that time is the only thing you cannot get more of. There is no such thing as a little bit of time. Remember that delegation is one of The Big Three Career Killers. Work hard and improve your delegation skills every day. It's how you grow as a leader and it's how you grow leaders. Only do what only you can do. Use the steps to delegation. Make sure that you're leveraging your time and your resources as much as you can to achieve your goals and to achieve incredible, lasting success.

Key Takeaways

In the space below, write your Key Takeaways from this chapter.

KEYS TO ORGANIZING

Identify Your Resources

* Time
* People
* Money
* Materials & Equipment
* Facilities & Technology
* Education & Training

Define & Communicate Goals

* What's the goal?
* Who's the Leader?

Roles & Responsibilities

* Published Organization Chart
* Goal Boss Teams
* Key Metrics
* Goals
* Team Problem Solving

goal boss

CHAPTER NINETEEN

Best. Meeting. Ever!

Meetings are like skiing. If you're not enjoying yourself, you are doing it wrong. Most of the time, meetings are not what happens in conference rooms. Most of the time, what goes on are gatherings. Unstructured conversations looking for a point. Remember that Harvard Business Review report stating that sixty five percent of senior managers surveyed feel that meetings keep them from completing their own work. Seventy one percent said meetings are unproductive and inefficient! Seventy one percent! How valuable would it be if your meetings were focused, productive, and perhaps even fun?

The fourth Key to Leadership is Controlling. Comparing performance to objectives and taking appropriate action. That is exactly what happens in a Goal Boss Meeting.

Monthly Goal Boss Meetings are the single most effective strategy to engage your team and drive results in your organization. Unlike other meetings you have, your Goal Boss Meeting is an interactive, well-planned collaboration amongst the best and the brightest in your organization. Everyone participates and contributes in measurable, meaningful ways. Goal Boss Meetings start on time and they end on time. Best of all, when you leave a Goal Boss Meeting, you know why you were there and you know what is expected of you next. In a word, Goal Boss Meetings are about Controlling.

Roster

Choosing the right people for your Goal Boss Team is imperative. Put simply, the goal of this meeting is to get stuff done. To improve the Key Metrics of the business with the help and collaboration of your team. Every single person in the room should be able to make immediate and direct contributions to that goal. Goal Boss Teams consist of the highest performing, hardest working members of the organization.

The question to answer when forming your Goal Boss Team is; who do you need to achieve your goals? For the most part, your roster will follow the org chart. For example, the CEO of a company would usually have the Chief Financial Officer, Chief Operating Officer, VP of Sales and Marketing, Chief People Officer, and Chief Technology Officer on their Goal Boss Team. There will be times, however, when one of your impact players does not report directly to you. If you cannot achieve your goals without that person, however, they belong on your Goal Boss Team.

Size matters. Our research has shown that a team size of five, plus or minus two, gets the best results. A Goal Boss Meeting with fewer than three people often fails to achieve critical mass. Because the meeting is a highly focused team event, the absence of a full team prevents actual teamwork from occurring. The give-and-take, information sharing, and the energy created by a group doesn't exist in teams of less than three people. For teams of two people, using the Goal Boss Coaching model, or joining a Goal Boss Mastermind Team are both highly effective alternatives. At the other end of the spectrum, when team size exceeds seven or eight members, difficulties with time management, focus and team cohesion crop up. Even for experienced facilitators, it can be a challenge to manage a tightly choreographed meeting with more than eight high performing people at one time. There are instances when team sizes must exceed seven members. When this happens, give serious thought to hiring professional facilitator for your Goal Boss Meeting.

Whom do you rely on to get things done? When choosing members of your Goal Boss Team, find your A-Players. Those people who do outstanding work and also exemplify the organization's values. Values are every bit as important as performance. Adding an OBT or a hanger-oner to your Goal Boss team sends the wrong message and hampers the team's ability to succeed. You don't need the best people nearly as much as you need the right people. Everyone on your Goal Boss Team should be expected to give one hundred percent focus, effort, and attention to the team. Choose your team carefully.

Ground Rules

Meetings without ground rules are not meetings. Chapter two discusses ground rules in detail. Review that section before your first Goal Boss Meeting because you will need your ground rules. Post your ground rules on the wall in your conference room or meeting space so you can refer to them throughout the meeting. Even the best teams can get off track now and then. Having ground rules in plain sight allows the facilitator of the meeting to refocus the team and keep the meeting on track. At the start of your Goal Boss Meeting, review the ground rules one at a time.

Below are the ground rules you can expect to see when a Goal Boss Certified Coach is your facilitator. We have chosen these rules because they keep the team focused, the conversation on point, and at the same time, they allow sufficient latitude in terms of conversation and creativity. As you evolve the style of your own Goal Boss Meetings, these ground rules will make a solid start.

Confidentiality - What's said in this room stays in this room.

Teamwork - Individuals go fast, but teams go far.

Everyone Participates - You are in the room because the team needs your best thinking.

No Sidebars - Everyone in a Goal Boss Meeting is there for a reason. Stay focused and show respect for your teammates.

Airplane Mode - Turn off your electronics. This is not the time for doing busy work or catching up.

Candid, Timely Feedback - Be prepared to have your ideas respectfully challenged in the best interest of the team.

Manage Time. Ruthlessly - Goal Boss Meetings start on time and they end on time.

No Rabbit Holes - Focus and discipline are the key to high performing teams.

Attack the Problem, not the Person - Keep your feedback focused on solving problems rather than criticizing people.

Important Things Can't Be Discussed Comfortably - This meeting is not meant to be restful. Be prepared to discuss uncomfortable topics and stretch yourself mentally and perhaps even emotionally. High performing teams give one hundred percent.

Lean In & Have Fun - Give it your all. Check your ego at the door and enjoy the opportunity to be in a room full of A Players!

Successes

After a quick review of the Ground Rules, kick off your Goal Boss Meeting by collecting and writing down all the successes your team has enjoyed in the last thirty days. Remember one of your ground rules is that everyone participates. Go around the room and collect as many successes as you can. Write each success on a flip chart, one success per line. Write successes using a green marker if you have one.

As the facilitator of the meeting, your job is to bring out the best thinking and participation of everyone in the room. When making lists like this one you may use the "What else" technique we use in coaching sessions.

Here is how a typical "What else?" exchange might go in a typical Goal Boss Meeting.

Coach: Any other successes, team? What else?

Client: Geez, I'm not sure.

Coach: Not sure? What else?

Client: Oh, I don't really know. There's not much else.

Coach: Not much else? What else?

Client: I'm pretty sure that's it for successes.

Coach: That's it? What else?

Client: Well there is this one thing that's got me really excited...

In high school, I had a teacher who often said, "I don't know is not an answer!" I disagree. I don't know is certainly an answer.

But, it is a lazy answer. In a Goal Boss meeting never settle for 'I don't know.' The first four times someone gives you that answer, use the "What else" technique to make absolutely sure you get every single success from the last thirty days listed. It is important to take the time to celebrate the successes of the team, both large and small. Listing successes in this fashion is also a potent means of stimulating creativity and teamwork at the start of the meeting.

After you gather and list all the successes of the team from the last thirty days, take the time to post your charts on the wall. You and the team will refer back to these at different times during the remainder of the meeting.

Concerns

The process for listing concerns is the same as that for successes. What issues or problems are keeping you up at night? What questions or controversies are standing between you and achievement of your goals. Maybe sales are down for the month. Perhaps you have had difficulty filling a particular job or role on the team. Any situations or issues that are of concern to the team should be surfaced and written down in the Concerns section of your Goal Boss Meeting.

As the facilitator of the meeting, this may be a good time to remind the team that one of the ground rules is important things can't be discussed comfortably. Most people shy away from difficult conversations. High performing teams never do. If there is an issue with a teammates performance, or an uncomfortable change in the organization, this is the time to get it out on the table. Concerns hidden or ignored will fester and grow. Acknowledging the elephant in the room can be a powerful tool to increase communication and set the stage for solving problems and achieving goals. Write concerns on your flipchart using red ink. This will make it easy to find and reference the concerns of the team throughout the meeting.

For teams that are new to the Goal Boss Meeting process, listing concerns is often the easy part. Even so, be sure to go around the room and use the "What else" technique at least five times to be certain you have collected all of the concerns of the team. After you are certain you have all the teams' concerns listed on your charts, it is time to assign ownership.

Using a black marker, go back through the listed concerns and assign an owner to each one. The rules of ownership are these: The owner of a concern is not necessarily responsible for solving the problem or addressing the issue personally. Instead, the owner of the concern is the person who is responsible for understanding the status of the concern, and having an overview of the situation. If someone entered the room and asked, "Who do I see about that concern?", the owner would be that person. The second rule is that ownership of a concern can only be assigned to someone who is in the room at the time ownership is being assigned. It neither productive nor fair to assign ownership of a concern to someone who might be unaware of the concern in the first place and who assuredly does not know the concern is being discussed in a confidential meeting of which they are not a part. Listing and assigning ownership to concerns is seldom comfortable. Goal Boss Teams are not focused on staying comfortable during this meeting. This is where important things are discussed and important things often cannot be discussed comfortably.

Kudos

Who has done something amazing for the organization in the past thirty days? In a Goal Boss Meeting, the purpose of Kudos is to foster a culture of recognition. This is achieved by identifying between one and five people in the organization who have made outstanding contributions within the last thirty days. People on the Goal Boss Team should not be nominated for kudos in this part of the meeting because the purpose of Kudos is to benefit the larger team, the whole organization. Here is an example.

A member of the Goal Boss Team, Rhonda, is the Chief Sales Officer. She has decided to nominate Jane for Kudos this month. Jane came in to work over the weekend to help the accounting team complete the sales commission reports for last quarter. Jane was not asked to help with this task, nor is accounting in her job description. Jane is part of the marketing department. Rhonda feels that Jane went above and beyond the call of duty to help her teammates even though there was nothing in it for her.

On hearing the story of Jane and the sales commission reports, the Goal Boss Team agrees that Jane deserves kudos this month. It is important, when recognizing behaviors to use verbs. Everyone knows that Jane is a team player. She goes the extra mile and has a winning attitude. While all of these things may be true of Jane, general qualities - adjectives - are difficult to quantify. Verbs, on the other hand, such as "helped complete the commission reports," and "came into work over the weekend," are easily observable behaviors. Kudos should be given based on observed, desirable behaviors. The reason for this becomes clear when you know how a Goal Boss Team lets people know that they have earned Kudos.

On a flipchart in the room, the facilitator of the meeting writes Kudos at the top of the sheet. Then, Jane Doe. Below that, a brief description of what Jane did. Your team may have a few other people to nominate for Kudos as well. Write them all down. Goal Boss Certified Coaches will use a purple colored marker to list Kudos on flipcharts. Purple is an important color.

Finally, each Kudos recipient is assigned an owner. The Kudos Owner must be a member of the Goal Boss Team and they must be present at the meeting. To qualify as a Kudos Owner, they should not be the direct supervisor of the Kudos nominee. They cannot be Jane's boss. Chances are, Jane's boss has already thanked Jane for the good work. Part of the special nature of earning Goal Boss Kudos is the practice of having someone from a completely different department take the time to recognize the Kudos nominee. Here is how that that might go.

Cliff, the Chief Technology Officer, volunteers to deliver Kudos to Jane. Cliff doesn't know Jane very well at all. They work at different ends of the building and rarely interact. After the Goal Boss Meeting, Cliff sends a meeting invitation to Jane. He schedules fifteen minutes in her office. Cliff shows up for the meeting, on time, and says to Jane, "Jane, you may know that I'm on the Executive Goal Boss Team for the company. I wanted to let you know that at our monthly meeting yesterday, Rhonda told all of us about how you came into work over the weekend to help closeout the commission reports for the sales team. Everyone in the meeting was impressed with your sense of teamwork and your willingness to go the extra mile. I just wanted to take a few minutes to thank you personally and let you know that your contribution was noticed and appreciated by the whole executive team. If you don't mind, I would like to send out an email to the whole company and thank you publicly. Would that be okay?"

Question: How does Jane feel after the CTO makes a trip to her office to thank her for her contribution? She feels wonderful.

Question: How does the rest of the company feel when they read the public thank you email? They feel happy for Jane, and they wonder how they can get that kind of recognition for themselves.

Recognition is the single most powerful motivator of people in the workplace. Goal Boss Kudos is a highly efficient means of recognizing high performing members of the team throughout your organization. It is also fun for everyone involved.

Key Metrics

After the fun of Kudos, it is time to get down to brass tacks. Reporting on Key Metrics is very straightforward. Each member of the team has their own Key Metrics to report on. Going around the room, teammates report their Key Metrics results as follows:

Key Metric Name, target value, actual value, variance. Sometimes the news is good, sometimes it is not so good. Reporting out on Key Metrics is just that. Reporting. Don't waste time after each bit of information to brag or make excuses. Just the facts. After going around the room, everyone on the team knows exactly where the entire organization stands. Spreadsheets or the Goal Boss app are both excellent ways to keep track of your Key Metrics on a monthly basis.

If someone on the team has a clarifying question about one or more of your Key Metrics, answer briefly and succinctly. Remember. No Rabbit Holes is one of our ground rules.

Goals

On an established Goal Boss Team, everyone comes to the meeting with their goal achievement recorded from last month and their goals for next month already written for review by the team. In the same order that the team reported out on Key Metrics, you now go around the room to report out on Goals. Each member of the team has their own Goal Scorecard. You can create a scorecard using spreadsheets or you can use the Goal Boss app. Everyone on the team reports out on their goals as follows.

First, the total number of goals set last month, total goals achieved, goal achievement percentage. Next, read each goal as written and the goal status of done or not done. If the goal is not done, the facilitator will ask if it is still a goal. If so, they will ask for a revised due date. High performing teams have a goal achievement rate of about eighty percent. Eighty percent goal achievement tells us that you and your team that you are setting challenging goals without being unrealistic. When goal achievement falls below eighty percent, that indicates something is amiss. Again, briefly answer any questions your teammates may have, then move on to your goals for next month.

Show up at the meeting with between three and five SMART Eulogy Goals with Goal Certainty of about eighty percent. Expect your facilitator and your teammates to challenge you on all counts, and remember you are expected to challenge your teammates. The due date for your Goal Boss Meeting goals should be on or before your next scheduled Goal Boss Meeting. Before you finalize your goals for next month, double check the list of Concerns that you own. Are your current goals going to address any of those Concerns? If not, consider revising a goal or adding another. Every goal you set should directly impact one or more of your Key Metrics and or your Concerns. That is what the "R" in SMART stands for. Relevant.

When you have gone around the room and the whole team has reported out on goals, you compile your team goal scorecard to make sure you are performing at the level you expect of yourselves and your organization expects of you.

Team Problem Solving

Goal Boss Meetings are built on the Pareto Principle. Minute for minute, the time you invest in this meeting can yield five times the results you get from other activities. Team Problem Solving is the twenty percent of your Goal Boss Meeting that can yield eighty percent of its value. Team Problem Solving is extreme productivity. Extreme communication. Extreme leadership. Make sure to do at least three Team Problem Solving sessions at every Goal Boss Meeting. Review the team problem solving details we covered earlier, and keep in mind these basic guidelines.

1. State "How to" question with background and facts (1 min)
2. Questions from the team (2 min)
3. Write suggested action steps (5 min)
4. Stop and jot selected action steps (2 min)

You can find Team Problem Solving worksheets and the app at www.goalboss.com. This part of the meeting is easy to skip. Don't skip it. High performing teams step up and do this work regularly.

Key Takeaways

Before you close the meeting, gather up Key Takeaways, or KTAs, as we call them. Simply write KTA's on a fresh sheet of flipchart paper using a purple marker and work your way around the room. What is your Key Takeaway from the meeting? The one thing you learned, thought of, noticed, or felt more than anything else. Record Key Takeaways from everyone on the team. As the facilitator, write your Kay Takeaway last, then read back all of the Key Takeaways out loud.

Schedule Next Meeting

Make sure everyone in the room knows the date for next month's Goal Boss Meeting. Remember Pareto. Everyone on the team is expected to attend at least eighty percent of all Goal Boss Meetings. Do not fall into the trap of cancelling or delaying because one person cannot attend. Keep the schedule. That is what high performing teams do.

Running successful Goal Boss Meetings is an uncomplicated process. Transforming your organization into a high performing team is not about talent. It is about teamwork, hard work, communication, delegation and time management. Everything you need is right here in this book. Everything in this book is right here in this meeting.

Key Takeaways

In the space below, write your Key Takeaways from this chapter.

_____

_____

_____

_____

_____

_____

_____

_____

_____

_____

_____

_____

_____

_____

CHAPTER TWENTY

Keys to Controlling

Controlling is comparing performance to objectives and taking appropriate action. That is what controlling is all about. You've now learned how to identify your Key Metrics, set impactful goals, and solve problems with your team. Those are the core skills of the Goal Boss Leadership System. Setting up your Goal Boss Team and conducting engaging Goal Boss Meetings will take you and your teammates to the next level and beyond. More on that later. Now, let's clearly understand the Keys to Controlling.

Clearly Define Goals

The first question to ask yourself when we start anything: What's the goal? You want to define your goals and be certain they are aligned with the vision, mission and values that your business is based on. Make sure that your goals support your strategic and operating plans. Your strategic plan is the thing that we develop once a year toward the end of the year. It is a one-day or two-day session that you can run on your own and we coach you on how to do it, or you can have a Goal Boss Certified Coach come and work with you. The operating plan is also known as the One Page Plan. When you are setting goals check those documents and ask yourself if your goal is relevant to your strategic and operating plans. Are you setting out to do something that is going to make a difference to your Key Metrics? Track your goals in Goal Boss. It is a whole lot easier to use Goal Boss than a bunch of emails and other bespoke goal tracking documents.

Implement a Measurement System

Use Goal Boss to track goal achievement. When you report on your goal at a monthly Goal Boss meeting, your facilitator will ask a couple of simple questions: is the goal achieved or not achieved, yes or no? If it is 'yes' that's great, if it is not, is it still a goal? If it is still a goal what is the new due date? This simple goal achievement process is built right into Goal Boss.

Goal Boss is your goal score card for each month. It shows how many of your goals you achieved measured as a percentage. Shoot for eighty percent goal achievement overall. That is how you know you are pushing hard enough, not laying back, challenging yourself, and coming through for your team. Every month the Goal Boss meeting is a mini-performance review. At the end of year when you have your formal performance review there will be no surprises because every month we are keeping score and measuring performance using Goal Boss, both at the individual level and organizational level.

Communicate Expectations.

Let people know what you expect and what to expect. These are the tools, strategies and techniques to use in communicating your expectations to your team and your organization.

Ground Rules, Policies and Procedures

We talked about this at the very beginning of the book: what are the ground rules, what is expected of you, what are the rules of engagement in this environment? Ground rules. Use the Communication Loop to make sure everyone understands your ground rules.

Written Role Descriptions

Let people know what you expect. How do you do that? Written role descriptions. Everyone in the organization must have a current role description that matches what they currently do.

90-Day Onboarding Plan

I cannot say enough about the importance of the 90-day onboarding plan. When someone joins your organization, they want to know what it takes to be successful in this environment. Visit goalboss.com to download our Rapid Values Onboarding™ template. This will show you how to give your people the tools they need to be successful in your organization. A 90-day onboarding plan includes 30-day, 60-day, 90-day goals. What are your expectations of the new employee? What can they expect of you? What is their learning style, what is their behavioral style? Give them a Goal Boss DISC assessment so you know the best way to communicate with them, and they know the best way to communicate with you. All of that is in the 90-day onboarding plan. These drives performance and creates a culture where communication and accountability are the norm. This is what high performing teams do. Without taking these steps you cannot expect to get the results of a high performing team.

Scheduled Objective Performance Reviews

Monthly Goal Boss meetings are scheduled objective performance reviews. Anyone who is a member of a Goal Boss team sets goals that they own, they define key metrics that they own, and they are accountable. When you communicate expectations in this way everyone in the organization commits to being in charge of their own performance, being owners of their own performance, having responsibility for themselves. You are not pushing anymore, you are leading from the front.

Candid, Timely Feedback

A key question you can ask your people is, "Are you open to some feedback?' When you do ask that question, the answer should be yes. Then you can give that person feedback. When giving kudos to teammates, make sure to use verbs instead of adjectives. When you give someone feedback, make objective observations of their behavior. Don't ask, "Why are you so lazy and late for work all the time?"

That approach is not productive. To address tardiness, it would be more productive to say, "I noticed that you are not arriving at work on time. Is there something I can do to help?"

It is the exact same issue but what you are doing is framing the issue so that you are both on the same side of the table. You are attacking the problem and not the person.

Observable & Objective

When you give candid, timely feedback make sure that it is understandable by everyone in the conversation. Use the communication loop: can you play that back to me so I know I did a good job of communicating it? My expectation is that you are here at 8 o'clock in the morning. Can you play that back to me so that I know I did a good job of explaining it?

Timely and Accurate

If somebody is late for work today and you need to give them feedback about it, give them feedback about it today. Do not wait a month and say, "Oh well a month ago you were late." You make it personal if you wait a long time to give someone that feedback. Timely and accurate feedback gets positive results. Giving corrective feedback may not be comfortable but it is an important behavior of a high performing team.

Measure. Adjust. Repeat.

That is what Goal Boss is all about. That is what Key Metrics are all about, and that is what setting goals is all about. High performing organizations and teams constantly measure performance and take action to improve results. High performing teams are always finding ways to improve results.

Compare Target and Actual Results

Remember in the Goal Boss Team meeting chapter when we looked at our team. We could compare the target results to the actual results, and based on that information we set goals to move the needle on the things that matter most. Those Key Metrics. Investigate and understand variances. If it is not what it should be, wonder why? Get really curious. Dig all the way to the bottom of it and figure out why there are variances if your numbers aren't what they should be.

Attack the Problem Not the Person

We cannot stress this enough. Always bring compassion, generosity, and kindness to your team. But do not let things get personal when it comes to performance or behaviors. Attack the problem not the person.

Take Appropriate Action

The definition of controlling is to compare objectives to performance and take appropriate action. Said differently, measure what matters, then change what's measured.

Team Problem Solving

Every Goal Boss Meeting is an opportunity to practice Team Problem Solving. Be an expert at that and you will get things done like rocket scientists get things done.

SMART Goals with Clear Ownership

Specific, measurable, attainable, relevant, and time-bound. We have been through the goal setting process several times because it is so important. Make sure that you set SMART goals and make sure that one goal has one owner.

Monthly Goal Boss Meetings

Conduct regular Goal Boss meetings every month. Success is a process not an event. No one single thing is going to make your team a high performing team. High performing teams do controlling, high performing teams do everything detailed in this book. Do it over and over and over again, and you will get better and better and better. Push yourself and your team. Challenge yourself because you know that these are the actions that transform your organization into a high performing team.

Key Takeaways

In the space below, write your Key Takeaways from this chapter.

_____

_____

_____

_____

_____

_____

_____

_____

_____

_____

_____

_____

_____

_____

KEYS TO CONTROLLING

Clearly Define Goals
- Aligned with Vision, Mission, Values
- Support Strategic and Operating Plans
- Tracked in Goal Boss

Implement Measurement System
- Key Metrics
- Goal Achievement
- Individual Performance

Communicate Expectations
- Written Role Descriptions
- Ground Rules, Policies and Procedures
- 90-Day Onboarding Plan
- Scheduled, Objective Performance Reviews

Candid, Timely Feedback
- Observable & Objective
- Understandable by all teammates
- Timely & Accurate

Measure, Adjust, Repeat
- Compare Target & Actual results
- Investigate & Understand Variances
- Attack the Problem, Not the Person

Timely, Appropriate Action
- Team Problem Solving
- SMART Goals with Clear Ownership
- Regular Goal Boss Meetings

CHAPTER TWENTY-ONE

Coaching in Goal Boss

As you continue to develop your leadership skills, you will need better and sharper tools to make sure your people continue to grow and thrive. The most effective strategy you can implement is a consistent, monthly one-on-one coaching relationship with each of the people you lead.

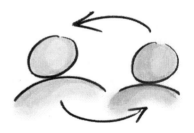

The Goal Boss Coaching Process is an effective way to discuss the issues and goals that are important to the people you lead. Their personal and professional development path should be aligned with the needs and goals of the organization. The Goal Boss Coaching Process helps you manage coaching in a way that is efficient and grows the leadership relationships you have with your team.

The big secret that professional coaches never want you to learn is that effective coaching is a skill that can be taught and learned. Effective coaching is not a talent that you are born with. Skillful coaching comes from the consistent application of proven techniques. Being an inspired coach is less important than being a consistent coach with a proven system. Lighting up the room with inspirational thoughts, feelings, and stories is far less important than following a set of proven guidelines. The Goal Boss System gives you exactly the coaching guidelines you need to start coaching your direct reports as soon as you finish reading this chapter. Effective coaching comes from a proven process. Let's review the steps of that process now.

Successes

A Goal Boss coaching session begins like a Goal Boss Team Meeting. As the coach, ask your client to list their successes for the past thirty days, or since your last coaching session. What has gone well? What are some of the good things that have happened in the last thirty days or so? If it is your first session ask about the past thirty days. If it is your second or subsequent session with this client, ask what has gone really well since the last time you met together? How much detail you go into for successes is between you and your client. The point of listing things in a coaching session is not so much to create a detailed historical record, but to start kicking ideas, thoughts and feelings loose in the mind of your client. Things that your client, and you, can be proud of.Don't be too quick to let your client off the hook. A simple coaching tactic when asking for a list of items is to simply ask, "What else?" By asking what else, you let the client know that they are not done with this particular subject. If you are new to coaching, remember to ask, "What else," at least five times for every section. Successful coaches never let you off the hook. Successful coaches make you finish. Do not let your coaching clients off the hook.

Try not to talk. As a coach, use the fewest words possible during the coaching session. Coaching works best when the client does most of the work. For example, when your making lists of successes, or making other lists ask, "What else," and then stop talking. Not talking, also known as listening, is a surprisingly difficult skill to master. Skillful coaches are quite good at not talking.

Concerns

The next list to get from your client is their list of concerns from the last thirty days, or since your last coaching session. Why would you ask for concerns? As the coach, you want to surface those things early on, and write them down. Remember to ask, "What else?"

Here is how a typical "What else?" exchange might go in a typical Goal Boss coaching session.

Coach: Any other concerns? What else?

Client: Geez, I'm not sure.

Coach: Not sure? What else?

Client: Oh, I don't really know. There's not much else.

Coach: Not much else? What else?

Client: I'm pretty sure that's it for concerns.

Coach: That's it? What else?

Client: Well there is this one thing that's got me really worried...

Bingo! If you ask someone the same question five times in a row, you are going to get more answers, and you are going to bring more value to the conversation. If you repeat the last few words of what they just said, they will elaborate.

Can that be awkward? Yes. Is it annoying? Perhaps. Your job as a coach has nothing to do with keeping things comfortable or pleasing. Your job is to coach. Ask the hard questions early, often, and over and over.

In all sorts of conversations, coaching conversations, teaching conversations, sales conversations, it is not until the fifth time you ask an important question that you get a good answer. The first three or four times, you are apt to get what we call a throw away answer. Something quick and easy the client may say to get herself off the hook. People do it because it works. Don't you give up. Ask "What else?" five times, every time. After you have asked what else five times and still have nothing, move on and be comfortable that you have all of the information you need.

Best Part of the Month

What was the best part of your month? One-on-one coaching works best when it is done monthly. More often than that and you are wasting time. Less often than that, and you lose momentum. So, ask what was the best part of the month? Of all the successes you listed earlier, what was the best thing that happened for your client this month?

When you ask your client "what was the best part of the month," you might stop them in their tracks a little bit, because people are not usually ready to answer specific questions. When you ask someone that question, they must catalog, sort, and order all of the events that have happened in the last thirty days. They have to think about everything that has happened. Once they have created the list in their head, they have to categorize and prioritize their experiences so they can recognize the single best part of the month. While your client is preparing their best part of the month answer, they are assigning a value to all their other experiences from the same time period. By asking this question, you help your client to bring all of their experience into the context of high performance, of getting things done, achieving goals, being successful. The more often a client does this, the more often they are asked this question, the more skillful they become at categorizing, sorting and assigning value to their experiences. Answering this question helps your client become more aware and more adept at making sense of their world. Living in a world that makes more sense brings more confidence and higher emotional intelligence.

The best part of the month question is an important question to ask. Do not let the person you are coaching off the hook. Wait for them to give you the answer. Never settle for "Oh, geez, I don't know, it's kind of everything." Find out. What was the best part of the month? Get a specific incident, a specific event that happened for that person during the month that was the best.

Worst Part of the Month

What was the worst part of the month? When you ask your client this question, the same process goes on in their mind. This time they get to deal with their negative experiences from the month. Your client has an opportunity here to categorize their failures, their disappointments, and missed opportunities. Someone made a mistake or the client made a mistake and didn't manage to learn from it, they lost a client, they lost a friend. Be prepared for anything here, and remember you are not a therapist! You are not there to diagnose or fix problems. Listen and record only. Let your client think of all of the things they did this month. All the events and experiences from this month that were not good, and put them in context. Especially the context of the best thing that happened this month.

As a dad, I ask my kids this my question every day. What was the best part of your day, what was the worst part of your day?

My kids know by now that it's going to happen. So, they prepare for best-part-worst-part subconsciously throughout the day. They know when they see me at the end of the day I am going to ask.

That conversation makes for a productive relationship. When you ask those questions, you are not stepping over any line. You are just asking good questions. Questions that have meaning, that let the other person do the thinking and contribute to the conversation. Asking what was the best part of your month and what was the worst part of your month is critically important to the coaching process.

Goals and Key Metrics

Goal Boss Coaching is designed to work either as a standalone process or as part of the larger Goal Boss Leadership System. If you and your coaching client are both members of the same Goal Boss Team, you will be able to see and share your business goals and team Key Metrics, and have a deeper conversation about those during your coaching session.

Ask your client to share goals that have a due date on or before the day of your coaching session. Which goals should be done by now? Like a Goal Boss Meeting your client reports the status of their goals efficiently, objectively, and without excuses. The process for reporting on goals follows:

1. Read the goal as written. For example, "I will open fifty new reseller accounts by January 15th."
2. Report the goal status, which is either Done, or Not Done.
3. If the goal is Not Done, ask your client, "Is it still a goal?"
4. If the goal is still a goal, ask your client, "What is the new Due Date?

Reporting on Goal achievement should be kept objective and professional to guard against creating an environment where your client feels obligated or allowed to prepare excuses. The coaching conversation is not about judgment. Keeping to the goal reporting script also helps you manage time. Excuses tend to be variable in length and detail. Even if hearing excuses was productive, it is not practical to try and schedule time to hear excuses.

Key Metrics reporting works the same way goal reporting does. Before the coaching session begins, your client should prepare both their both personal and business Key Metrics results. The client reads the Key Metric name, target value, actual value, and the variance.

For example, "Reseller Sales Volume. Target is fifty thousand, actual is fifty-five thousand, and the variance is five thousand above target, which is good."

As the coach, you should listen quietly to the results, good or bad, and take it all in. Avoid expressing approval or disapproval at this stage of the session.

After you are caught up on past Goals and Key metrics, ask your client to read their goals for next month. As the coach, your job is to ask the client if these are SMART goals. Ask which of their Key Metrics each goal is designed to impact, and how. Ask your client what their level of goal certainty is for each goal, keeping in mind that a goal certainty level of eighty percent is optimum. Ask your client why eighty percent goal certainty is desirable. Remember that a high performing member of a high performing team will usually have between three and seven powerful, impactful, challenging goals every month. If your client does not have at least three, take a little time and have them set one or two more goals. Ask your client what a Eulogy Goal is, and why they are so powerful. Good goals are crucial to high achievement. Make sure your client works hard at this.

Kudos

Kudos in personal coaching works a little bit different than kudos in a Goal Boss Meeting. The point here is to allow the coach an opportunity to give kudos to the client. The reason that you as the coach should give kudos as part of the coaching session, is because your client needs to know you are participating in the coaching session beyond just writing down lists, and the client needs to see you demonstrate that you care. If you know this part of the session is coming, and you know you are expected to recognize a specific positive behavior, you are going to pay close attention. Remember, as the coach it is appropriate to give kudos about a particular specific behavior or achievement. Not something vague like, "You're a great guy, you really go the extra mile."

Avoid generalizations when giving kudos. For kudos, work to call out behaviors and actions rather than qualities or features. Use verbs, not adjectives. Get into the habit of being specific about what people do right. Calling out the details of good behaviors reinforces those behaviors. For example, you might say, "You did an excellent job of explaining the why of best part of the month, worst part of the month. That is really going to be useful to the whole team. Great contribution."

Again, as the coach you need to prepare for this. You know this is coming. Because if you are not able to think of something positive to say off the top of your head, it could make for an awkward moment. Before the coaching session starts, prepare. Review the goals and key metrics of the person you are coaching. Look at your notes and the coaching report from the last session. Give this some thought because it is an important part of the job and the kudos can have a significant impact on the client's attitude and performance.

Feedback

Next, we give feedback to the person we are coaching. This is the opportunity to offer constructive criticism. We attack the problem not the person. Provide well intentioned feedback, and avoid expressing your feelings about what you have observed. Keep your feedback objective. An experienced coach attacks the problem, not the person. As the coach, when you illuminate an opportunity for improvement, or call attention to a behavior, do it in a non-emotional, objective, productive way. This section is short because the feedback section of a coaching session should be short. Don't dwell. Deliver your observations, listen to anything your client may have to say, and move on.

Key Takeaways

At the end of the coaching session come Key Takeaways. At Goal Boss, we often call them KTA's. This is your last list for the coaching session. Ask your client what their Key Takeaways were from the conversation. What were the most important things they learned?

Again, be sure to use "What else?" Ask five times. Imagine making these lists is like using a drink machine when you want a bottle of water. Push the button five times before you give up. We always push the button five times before we give up. That is how many times people try for something when they really want it.

You didn't push that button once and say, "Oh well, that was it," and walk away. You wanted that water. You pushed the button at least five times before you gave up. Do the same thing with "What else?" Ask "What else?" five times and you will get more information out of the conversation and you will bring more value to the conversation than the average coach ever would.

You can do amazing things with this. The extraordinary coach does ordinary things in a different order than most coaches. Asking "What else?" five times is one of those ordinary things that will produce extraordinary results.

Schedule the Next Session

Schedule your next coaching session before you leave this one. It will help you make and keep commitments to yourself and your team.

If you have eight direct reports, that is about eight hours a month you are going to invest in one-on-one coaching. At first glance you might think, I do not have another eight hours in a month.

But for every hour you invest in one-on-one coaching with someone on your team, you will save three or four hours of management time over the course of the month. This will save you time, and make your people far more productive.

You do not have to be a super coach to do this. Just follow the steps. You will save management time, particularly at the task level. You will shift conversations toward goals and achievement and you will help your people grow personally and professionally. Coaching is what leaders do.

Key Takeaways

In the space below, write your Key Takeaways from this chapter.

_____

_____

_____

_____

_____

_____

_____

_____

_____

_____

_____

_____

_____

_____

CHAPTER TWENTY-TWO

Keys to Leadership

May I just pause for a moment and offer my congratulations. You have reached the last chapter of this book. Nicely done! Leadership is about doing little things that add up to big things. Starting a book is something just about everyone has done. Finishing that book, especially a non-fiction business book, is a far less common occurrence. Finishing what we start is a leadership behavior. With that in mind, let's review the Keys to Leadership.

Coach!

The first key to leading is coaching. Be a coach. What does being a coach require? Most of all being a coach requires actively respecting your people. You respect them for who they are, for their capabilities, and you respect them for what they can become. See the potential in your teammates, and make sure they see it, as well.

Patience

We all make mistakes, we make mistakes as leaders, we make mistakes as teammates. We tend to mess things up on a pretty regular basis. That's ok, it's part of learning. As a leader, develop the skill of letting your people make mistakes. Learn to live with a little breakage now and then. The lessons learned from mistakes usually outweigh the cost of the mistake itself.

Respect

Value the individuals in the organization. As a coach, you value your people and they need to feel that. It needs to come through in no uncertain terms. People will walk through fire for you if they know you care.

Passion!

I hope that my passion for this topic and my passion for sharing this material with you has come through in every single page of this book. I bring a hundred percent of my passion to the work of leadership and training. For me, writing is an agonizingly painful process. If I did not love this work I would not do it. If you don't love what you are doing, quit. Go find something else to do. The thing you need above all is passion. At some point in your career as a leader, it is going to make more sense to give up, to quit, to give up on somebody else, than it will to keep going. The only thing that will keep you going is your passion for what you do. Make sure you love it. Demonstrate your passion in everything you do. Don't be afraid to look like a goofball. Don't be afraid to be silly. Don't be afraid to use the word passion. Use it and get the people around you using it as well.

Recognize Contributions

When somebody does something well, call it out. We discussed that in the chapter about Goal Boss Meetings. The

Kudos section of the meeting is one of the most important parts of the month for an organization. Recognize individual contributions and celebrate those individuals who contribute. Always remember that recognition is the number one motivator for people in an organization. Use it. It doesn't cost you anything and it will gain you everything.

Celebrate the Team

We value individuals, we celebrate the team. When your team has a win, when somebody on your team has a win, give them credit. Use the word "we" more than you use the word "I."

Embody the Vision

Remember your vision, mission, and values. Remember to have them written down. Everything you do as a leader is observed by the people you lead. Any time you exhibit a behavior that does not embody the vision, mission, and values of the organization, it will be noticed. And it will give everyone else permission to fall short in that area as well. So, embody the vision.

Be A Teacher!

Think about the people outside your family who have meant the most to you. Are any of them teachers? Coaches? Of course they are. The people who mean the most to us are those who change our perspective, who challenge our ideas, who force us to stretch and grow.

Knowledge Shared is Power

As a leader, you are also a teacher and there is no more solemn responsibility, no higher calling, than being a teacher. Knowledge shared is power. If you know something make sure that the people around you know it as well. Share what you know with others.

Learn from Mistakes

In every organization that I have led there has been a hard and fast rule that the only fatal mistake is hiding a mistake. You can mess up anything, as long as you are working hard for the team. When you do mess up, it is your obligation to bring that mistake to the team so that we can unpack it, learn from it, and move on to making new mistakes. Then we can learn from those mistakes. Embrace mistakes as the opportunities that they are.

Embrace Innovation

Great leadership comes from being around a while. I know what I'm talking about here. Younger people coming along have new ideas. Frankly, they are likely to come along with better ideas, innovations. Embrace innovation. Never get comfortable, never sit back. Never feel like you have got it all figured out. When somebody comes along with a new idea, when somebody wants to innovate, you should encourage that.

Become a Student of Leadership

Study leadership, read books about leadership, read books about leaders. Always be a student of leadership. Ask questions of other leaders. How do you do this? How did you handle that? Being a leader will bring you many and varied opportunities for insecurity, failure, falling short, disappointing people, messing up. That is perfectly fine. Just keep learning.

Courage!

Courage is what you get after doing the thing that you are afraid of. Your team depends on you to demonstrate courage in everything you do. This is a tall order. The good news is courage is a skill. You can learn courage. Here is how.

Lead with Confidence

Fake it till you make it. Take command and lead with confidence. If you are not sure whether we go right or left, your job as the leader is to make a decision and lead the team. Leaders take command and lead with confidence. Sometimes what your team needs is for you to make a decision and move. Know when to take command and lead with confidence.

Communicate the Vision Clearly and Often

Let your people know what your expectations are. Let your people know what you see as the future. Do not believe that since you presented the vision at the beginning of this month, you don't have talk about it anymore. Communicate the vision regularly and often. Use the communication loop. Can you play our vision back to me so I know I did a good job of communicating it? Get the team on the same page.

Live the Values

You must live the values if you want to lead. The values of Goal Boss are teamwork, hard work, communication, delegation, time management. If you ever see me doing something that does not look like at least one of those five things, you need to give me feedback right away because I live the values of my organization. Define your values, or borrow ours, and live up to them.

Take Risks

Often, we decide to move forward with ideas that are risky. That is why we lead in the industry. Before you start a new project or a new direction for your business or in your life, answer these questions: What could possibly go wrong? How could I prevent it from going wrong in the first place? If it did go wrong, how would I recover from it? Answer those questions and you will be able to take risks smartly. It is what leaders do.

Give it Away!

Share the Goal Boss system across your entire organization. It is not just for executives. High performing organizations foster leadership at every level.

Set Goals as A Team

Get Goal Boss meetings up and going. Give your managers a copy of this book so they can start coaching their direct reports today.

Trust Your People

When you delegate a task to someone, give them the task, step back and let them do it. Review the steps to delegation, make sure you are delegating expertly. Trust your people to get things done. It is the only way you and your organization can grow.

Measure Results

We went through this in the controlling section of this book. Measure results relentlessly, objectively. What gets measured gets managed. Measure what matters. Use Key Metrics.

Expect Excellence

You know what the people around you are capable of, so expect that. Don't settle for whatever somebody feels like doing today. Expect high performance and expect the team to live the organization's values as well. When you set expectations and communicate them clearly, people will step up. They will step up and they will thank you for it. No one ever thanked their coach or their boss for letting them off the hook. You don't help anybody by letting them off the hook. Expect excellence.

Teamwork!

Get your people involved in planning. Do not go behind closed doors and set the business plan for the year, come out and present it to the organization. People need to be involved in what they are doing. They need to be part of something bigger. When you don't involve the team in planning you are just issuing orders and that is not the same thing as leading. Involve the team in the planning.

Say "We" more than you say "I"

A lot more. In emails, do not ever use the word "I." When you use the word "we", you bring people into the conversation, you include others, you share responsibility, you share passion. You also teach generosity. So many things that can happen if you just strike the word "I" from your vocabulary.

Use Team Problem Solving

When something goes wrong invite everybody into the room and share it. People will clamor for the opportunity to share their ideas, to offer solutions. Team Problem Solving is a highly focused way to utilize that energy. When you use it in your organization, you will be more successful.

Add to the Ideas of Others

Add to ideas instead of taking away from them. This can be the difference between a high performing team and an average or an underperforming team. When somebody offers an idea in a high performing team the rest of the team will pitch in and offer suggestions to make that idea better. We have all been in the meeting where somebody says no that won't work because, or no that's a bad idea, or no that will never work. Don't diminish someone else's idea. It is not productive, and frankly, it is impolite. Establish a rule that you can only make a suggestion that will add to an idea, that will make an idea even better. These are the six keys to leadership. These are my six hopes for you and your organization.

I hope one day you and I will be able to work together in a Goal Boss event or workshop where we can share some time and have that conversation.

It has been a real privilege to share this book with you. I hope that you will reach out to us with any questions, any comments, and any feedback you may have. If there is anything we can do to be helpful, let us know.

Take action now that you have read this book. This is not over, this just started. We have built trainings, coaching, consulting, workshops, apps and software to support you in whatever ways we can. You can find out about all of that by visiting www.goalboss.com.

Key Takeaways

In the space below, write your Key Takeaways from this chapter.

_____

_____

_____

_____

_____

_____

_____

_____

_____

_____

_____

_____

_____

_____

_____

KEYS TO LEADERSHIP

Coach!
- Actively respect your people
- Patience
- Teacher, trainer, developer
- Value the individual

Passion!
- Demonstrate passion
- Recognize individual contributions
- Celebrate the team
- Embody the Vision

Teach!
- Knowledge shared is power
- Learn from mistakes
- Embrace innovation
- Become a student of leadership

Courage!
- Take Command and Lead with Confidence
- Communicate the vision clearly and often
- Live the values
- Take risks... smartly

Give it Away!
- Set goals as a team
- Trust your people
- Measure Results
- Expect excellence

Teamwork!
- Involve the team in planning
- Use the word "we" more than "I"
- A lot more
- Team Problem Solving
- Add to the ideas of others.

goal boss

Index

About the Author

Internet pioneer Will Pemble built and sold Web.com, one of the largest web hosts on earth. A serial entrepreneur, he has been building and growing businesses of all shapes and sizes for more than 25 years. In addition to Web.com, Will built and sold a national technical certification company, and one of the first Internet Service Providers in San Francisco.

Will's dynamic style, broad experience, and genuine enthusiasm for business bring out the very best in the leaders and teams he serves. As a facilitator and keynote speaker, Will's feedback scores consistently rank in the 94th percentile, setting him apart from industry colleagues and peers alike.

Will coaches his clients on leadership, team dynamics, strategic planning, scaling up, web strategy, product management, marketing, software development, and business operations.

75004659R00124

Made in the USA
San Bernardino, CA
23 April 2018